HOLDING ONTO HOPE

ESSAYS, SERMONS AND PRAYERS ON RELIGION AND RACE

VOLUME 4

C. ANTHONY HUNT

Holding On To Hope
Essays, Sermons, and Prayers on Religion and Race
Volume 4
by C. Anthony Hunt

The Rhodes-Fulbright Library series

ISBN: 978-1-55605-482-2

Ebook: 978-1-55605-481-5

WYNDHAM HALL PRESS

www.wyndhamhallpress.com

Printed in The United States of America

TABLE OF CONTENTS

INTRODUCTION AND ACKNOWLEDGMENTS

In 1903, the great scholar, W.E.B Dubois published the work, *The Souls of Black Folk*, in which he offered the seminal declaration that "the problem of the 20th century is the problem of the color line." It is the observation, some 117 years later, among many – including myself - that Dr. Dubois's observation holds into another century, and that indeed, the problem of the 21st century remains the problem of the color line.

It is the sense here that the color line that Dubois envisaged was one that was clearly defined as a racial demarcation between black and white. He wrote less than forty years after the emancipation of the last black slaves in America on June 19, 1865, and what is now known as Juneteenth, and less thirty years after the nullification of virtually all of the relative gains of previously enslaved black Americans through the Reconstruction era (1863-1877). The color line still exists today, but it is a super-diverse, multi-colored, multi-lingual line that is blurred and broadened beyond mere blackness and whiteness. It is a color line of Hispanic, Asian, Middle Eastern, Near and Far Eastern, Indigenous Peoples, Blacks and whites.

Today's color line draws at intersections of race, class, gender, age, sexual orientation, bi-racialism, post-racialism, post-racism, immigration, interculturation and multiculturation. Reflected on today's color line is the fact that many people continue to languish in the disparate shackles and bondage of poverty, racism, sexism, lack of adequate and accessible healthcare, over-incarceration, and persistent concerns for their safety.

This volume is the fourth in a series of compiled essays, sermons and prayers that I've written and had published since 2006: *And Yet the Melody Lingers* (2006), *My Hope is Built* (2011), and *Stones of Hope* (2018). This, and the preceding volumes, speak to the times in which they were written, with the intersections of race, social, economic and political concerns, religious and human existence and striving.

As always, writing for me is done within the context of the community in which I live, love, work, minister and teach. And so, I am indebted to a large village of persons who have helped to shape and sharpen my thoughts, pushed and prodded my thinking, prayed for me, and encouraged and challenged me through this project.

I am forever grateful for my family – my wife Lisa, and our three children - Marcus (deceased), Kristen and Brian. I am grateful for our parents and grandparents who taught us, and on whose legacy we stand. I pray to honor and lean into their legacy in ways that the world will be made better for generations to come. I dedicate this volume to my ancestors – my parents, grandparents and great-grandparents on whose shoulders we stand today.

I am grateful for the people of Epworth Chapel United Methodist Church in Baltimore, Maryland where I have been privileged to serve as pastor since 2011, and where many of these sermons were preached, prayers prayed and essays formulated in our teaching and learning together. To my colleagues and students in the academic settings where I teach – St. Mary's Seminary and University, Baltimore, MD; Wesley Theological Seminary, Washington, DC; United Theological Seminary, Dayton, OH; and the Graduate Theological Foundation, Oklahoma City, OK – I am grateful for how you

8

continue to push my thinking, learning, teaching, research and writing.

The book's cover design contains a limited-edition painting by Poncho Brown, titled "Serve the Lord with Gladness". It was commissioned by Epworth Chapel United Methodist Church, Baltimore in 2006, and the original painting hangs in the main hall of Epworth Chapel.

It is my prayer that this volume will serve as a testament of hope (to coin a phrase from a book title by the late James Melvin Washington) and play a part for each person who will read it, in how we can hold onto hope in the days ahead. Dr. Martin Luther King, Jr. said that "hope is the refusal to give up despite overwhelming odds." May it be that we hold on to such hope.

SECTION ONE

1 - THE INVOCATION

(This prayer was offered for the Maryland State Senate and State of Maryland in Annapolis, MD on Tuesday, January 30, 2018.)

O God, from the rising of the sun, until the going down of the same, your name is worthy to be praised. We gather this morning as your people, and we are grateful for this opportunity that you've afforded for us to be together. We are grateful for the opportunities that you afford each of us to serve you and your people.

For the state of Maryland, we offer thanks to you. For our nation, we are grateful - for with all that is with us and before us, we know that you have been our help in ages past, and that you are our hope for days to come, and we know that your divine and mighty hand is on the nation and world as it has been in ages past. So, O God, we pray that you will continue to guide our feet as we run the race that has been set before us.

On this day, we pray that you will bless every hamlet and hill of this great state. Bless every community where your people live, every school where our children learn, the fields and grounds where they play, and the places where your people gather for work and leisure.

We pray especially for those across our state who bear the burdens of need and inequality due to lack of food, shelter, healthcare and substandard education. Help us to hear and heed the words of the ancient prophet to *"love kindness, do justice, and walk humbly with you."* (Micah 6:8)

For those who serve and lead this great state and nation in elective and appointive office – we pray that You will endow each with reasonable portions of vision, strength, wisdom, compassion, courage, integrity and justice. Help all of us to see all that we seek to accomplish in the light of your concern for the common good among us.

And let us realize the sentiments of yet another ancient prophet that *"justice would roll down as waters, and righteousness as a mighty stream."* (Amos 5:24)

Where dreams may be diminished and hopes frayed among us, help us to heed the sentiments of the great poet Langston Hughes to "hold fast to dreams, for when dreams die, life is a broken-winged bird that cannot fly." Indeed, where dreams may be diminished and hopes frayed among us, help us to "hold fast to dreams, for when dreams go, life is a barren field, frozen with snow." Amen.

2 - REV. DR. MARTIN LUTHER KING, JR. AND A LETTER TO AMERICA

(This was published as an article in the United Methodist Connection of the United Methodist Church, Fulton, Maryland in January, 2019)

This year (2019) marks the 90th anniversary of Rev. Dr. Martin Luther King, Jr.'s birth, and the 51st year after his assassination on April 4, 1968 in Memphis, Tennessee. As was the case in 1968, the nation and world today are fraught with social, economic, political and religious upheaval. Over the past several years, in the United States and across the globe, we have become more divided along various lines. In the U.S., the social and political division that we now experience is not really new, but it challenges our sense of normalcy in ways that it perhaps has not been challenged in the past.

In April of 1963, King wrote a letter to eight clergymen in Birmingham, Alabama which has come to be known as his Letter from Birmingham Jail, and on August 28th of the same year in Washington, DC, at the urging of gospel singer Mahalia Jackson, who encouraged him to "Tell them about the Dream, Martin!", King delivered the concluding recitation in what has come to be known as his "I Have a Dream" speech.

In the Birmingham letter and Washington, DC speech, King demonstratively outlined his singular vision for the realization of the *Beloved Community*. His assessment in the Letter from Birmingham Jail was that many churches and their leaders had been found wanting in the sphere of prophetic witness, and had too often remained complicit in their silence, and complacent in their inaction with regard to the need to address racial, social and economic oppression. He stated in the letter that "The church must be reminded that it is not the master or the servant of the state, but rather the conscience of the state. It must be the guide and the critic of the state." King further stated that, "There comes a time when silence becomes betrayal." In the "I Have a Dream" speech, he essentially described to the world his dream of the *Beloved Community*, when girls and boys of all races could play together and go to school together, and where people would be judged by the content of their character, and not by the color of their skin.

And so today, we might wonder what King would say if he were alive to write a letter to America. Here might be his letter to America in 2019:

My Dear American Sisters and Brothers,

I greet you in the agapic love of God in Christ, our Savior. I pray that all of you who now dwell in what is deemed to be the land of the free and the home of the brave find yourselves reasonably well. In looking back over the more than 50 years since my last public address at Mason Temple Church of God in Christ, in Memphis, Tennessee on the night of April 3, 1968, and my assassination on a balcony at the Lorraine Motel at 6:01 pm the following evening in that same city, much has occurred in America.

Much of the progress that was eventuated up to my death, as seen in the passing of national Civil Rights legislation in 1964, and Voting Rights and Immigration and Nationalization legislation in 1965 seemed to come to full fruition with the election of Barack H. Obama in 2008 as the 44th President of the United States, the first African American to hold the nation's highest office. And yet, subsequent years have seen the heightened emergence (or re-emergence) of evils such as racism, classism, sexism and misogyny, homophobia, and war and terror that have served to perpetuate and exacerbate division in much of society, and even in large segments of the churches. I remind you of what I deemed to be the "triplets of evil" – racism, classism/poverty and war – and that these, in many ways, continue to encumber America's progress as a nation.

In light of the challenges that confront you, I remind you to remain cognizant that, as I also shared during my life, there is a certain collective force among those of you who are committed to living the sentiments of the prophet Micah to "love kindness, do justice and walk humbly with God" (Micah 6:8). As I stated, "For when people get caught up with that which is right, and they are willing to sacrifice for it, there is no stopping point short of victory."

America, in light of all that now fractures you, like immigration at your borders and violence on many of your city's streets, I want to also remind you of how God has created each of you. The nature of humanity is that you have all been created by the same God, and God loves all of that which has been divinely created. Therefore, I remind you of the inherent worth, dignity and "somebodyness" in each of you. As I shared years ago, "all life is interrelated." All of life is part of a single process; all living things are interconnected; and all of you are sisters and brothers. Because all of you are interrelated, you cannot harm another person without harming yourself.

There is a great deal more that I could share, but I will conclude my letter by encouraging you to never give up hoping. Regarding hope, I remind you of my past sentiments that "hope is the refusal to give up despite overwhelming odds", and that hope is "animated and undergirded by faith and love." Remember, if you have hope, you have faith in something.

Never forget my words on the steps of the Lincoln Memorial in August 1963, in the dream that I shared with the nation on that day, that there would someday be "[hewn] out of the mountain of despair, a stone of hope."

My dream for you, America, remains the same as it was almost 56 years ago, that the Beloved Community will become a reality. As always, I pray that your best days and most blessed days are not behind you, but in your future.

With Agapic Love,
Your Brother Martin

3 - WE WERE MADE FOR THIS *(A Sermon)*

For you created my inmost being; you knit me together in my mother's womb. I praise you because I am fearfully and wonderfully made; your works are wonderful; I know that full well. My frame was not hidden from you when I was made in the secret place, when I was woven together in the depths of the earth. Your eyes saw my unformed body; all the days ordained for me were written in your book before one of them came to be. How precious to me are your thoughts, God! How vast is the sum of them! Were I to count them, they would outnumber the grains of sand— when I awake, I am still with you. (Psalm 139:13-18)

On this day 87 years ago (January 15, 1929) on a little avenue in Atlanta, Georgia, a baby was born who, through his 39 years of living, would change the course of humanity. Auburn Avenue – what has come to be affectionately called "Sweet Auburn Avenue" - was a place of human thriving.

On Auburn Avenue, Martin Luther King, Jr. learned about the importance of family, community and the church. He learned of the importance of each of these in not only understanding how to live, survive and thrive in life – but in understanding who he was as a person, created by the divine hand of God.

As a young black boy from the South, the most important thing that Martin Luther King, Jr. learned on "Sweet Auburn Avenue" was indeed that he was a child of the Most High God. He learned that race and the racism, that was real and insipid in his community and in communities surrounding his in Atlanta, were not the things that would ultimately define who he was, nor shape what he would become, or the contributions that he would make to improving humanity.

This is to say that King learned long before Rev. Jesse Jackson coined the phrase for popular and political consumption that "I am somebody" that he (King) was *"somebody"*. This realization that he was *"somebody"* – imbued in him in his youth - would carry Martin Luther King, Jr. from Auburn Avenue to Morehouse College, to Crozer Theological Seminary in Chester, Pennsylvania, to Boston University, and ultimately to Montgomery, Alabama to serve as pastor of Dexter Avenue Baptist Church. This realization of his *"somebodyness"* would serve to shape King's understanding of his own human dignity, and his insistence on the human dignity of all of humanity.

Indeed, King's signature contribution to the human project - beyond his accomplishments in Civil Rights, Voting Rights, protests, marches and sit-ins, and even beyond his constant articulation and yearning for the church and society to realize what it means to be the *Beloved Community* – was to remind us that whoever we are, we are *"somebody"*. King's seminal contribution to the world was a reminder that whatever our skin color, whoever are our parents, and from wherever we have come – we have dignity and worth in the sight of God.

This notion of our *"somebodyness"* is a critical theological and ethical claim in that it points to the notion that as each of us has been created in God's image – *imago dei* - we have inherent claims, in our very humanness in the image of God, to human dignity as seen in our concomitant claims to *justice, equality, fairness, peace and love.*

This is to say that our personhood is always to be understood within the context of the personhood of God – the creator, savior and sustainer of the world. Each of us is *"somebody"* in God's sight.

About 3000 years before King's birth in 1929, another King, David articulated this notion of *"somebodyness"* in terms that many people of faith have become familiar with when he talked to God and told God something that God already knew. David reminded God that God had *"fearfully and wonderfully made"* him.

What was David saying that could help us today? David's proclamation is a reminder to us - first and foremost - that just as God created David's inmost being – God did the same for you and me. Just as God knit David in his mother's womb - God did the same for you and me. Just as God's eyes saw David's unformed body, and knew David before David was known – God did the same for you and me.

David wrote this psalm in the context of reflection and retrospection. He wrote this song after having gone through some things… after having experienced some ups and downs in his life… after having gone through some valleys and vicissitudes that had come his way… after having encountered some people who had tried to take him out.

But in and through everything David had gone through – he could look back and give thanks to God who had fearfully and wonderfully made him, and who had kept him all along the way.

You and I have likewise been fearfully and wonderfully made by the same God who made David. God saw fit to reach down into human existence and make you and me as special editions of Godself – unique, particular, peculiar, special editions. We're fearfully and wonderfully made.

And just as God made us, God will keep us. *We were made for this.* And so, with whoever's in political office, we can rest assured that we were made for this. Whatever comes our way, we were made for this. Whatever the "this" is that we will have to face tomorrow – know that we were made for it.

What God desires for us is to do an extreme makeover in our lives. The apostle Paul, in his second letter to the Corinthian Church, said that *"if any person is in Christ Jesus, she or he is a new creation…old things have passed away, and behold all things have become new"* (2 Cor. 5:17).

Indeed, as God has made us for this, God in God's grace and mercy continues to mold us and remake us for all that is to come in life. It does not yet appear what God has in store for us. Paul intimated that, *"Eye has not seen, nor ear heard, nor entered into the heart of (persons), the things which God has prepared for those who love God"* (1 Corinthians 2:9).

Yes, indeed, *we were made for this*. The apostle Paul further intimated in his address to the church at Philippi that "*I can do all things through Christ who strengthens me"* (Philippians 4:13). And Paul reminded the church at Corinth that *"we are more than conquerors through Christ who loves us"* (Romans 8:37). *We were made for this!*

4 - A SENSE OF URGENCY (A Sermon)

I waited patiently for the Lord; he turned to me and heard my cry. He lifted me out of the slimy pit, out of the mud and mire; he set my feet on a rock and gave me a firm place to stand. He put a new song in my mouth, a hymn of praise to our God. Many will see and fear the Lord and put their trust in him. Blessed is the one who trusts in the Lord, who does not look to the proud, to those who turn aside to false gods. (Psalm 40:1-4)

For David, waiting had become a common, necessary and normal practice as we arrive at Psalm 40. For at least fifteen psalms - from Psalm 25 to Psalm 40 - David had sung about some of the realities involved in waiting on the Lord. David's "Songs in the Key of Life" here is a 15-chapter long-playing album – or in contemporary musical jargon, a mixtape - about waiting.

In Psalm 25:5 and 25:21, David began to compose this long-playing piece. In Psalm 37:7 and 37:39, David wrote another song about waiting – a song that intimated that he had waited on the Lord, and didn't get an immediate answer from God.

That's the nature of waiting isn't it? In learning how to wait, we learn how to deal with our own impatience. In learning how to wait, we learn how to deal with silence and delay with regard to our want and need, even in the face of God. The truth of the matter is that if we live long enough, we will learn that God doesn't always show up when we want God to show up in our lives. But we also learn that every delay that we encounter in life is not a denial.

David's waiting songs in Psalms 25-40, should be instructive for us today, and indeed encouraging for us in some way, as we live in the liminal time and space of waiting for change to come, waiting for God to show up in our individual and collective lives, and waiting for God turn some things around.

In reflecting on the current state of the church and world, a question brought to prominence in the 1980's by a well-known rhythm and blues singing group, Morris Day and the Time, comes to mind. Morris Day would typically begin the group's performances by asking a rhetorical question, *"What time is it?"* The question never elicited a verbal response because everybody who was listening knew that it was performance and party time. The question, *"What time is it?"* sheds light on the matter of the sense of urgency that is before us today.

On this week (in 2020) when we celebrate the life and legacy of Dr. Martin Luther King, Jr. (and the 91st anniversary of his birth), we are reminded that in the crucible of injustice and gradualism in America in the 1950's and 60's, King talked about the *fierce urgency of now*. In 1963, at the height of the Civil Rights movement, he said "We are now faced with the fact that tomorrow is today. We are confronted with the fierce urgency of now. In this unfolding conundrum of life and history, there *"is"* such a thing as being too late. This is no time for apathy or complacency. This is a time for vigorous and positive action."

These are days when we must continue to live with such a sense of a *fierce urgency of now*. With political discord, economic distress, violence, social unrest, and religious

21

uneasiness at the fore of our communal and spiritual conscience - we must live with such a *fierce urgency of now.*

With troubles and trials around us, with valleys and vicissitudes confronting us, with discouragement and despair that seems to abound – we must live with a *fierce urgency of now.* While we wait on God, we must continue to work for peace with justice; while we wait on the Lord, we must continue to love kindness and extend generosity; while we wait on God, we must continue to walk in faith and hope.

What might King say to the world if he were here today as it regards the sense of urgency that is ours? He might remind us that -

"The arc of the moral universe is long, but it always bends toward justice."

King might tell us that -

"True peace is not merely the absence of tension; it is the presence of justice."

And he might also remind us that -

With whatever we face today or tomorrow – the God who made heaven and earth is still able to keep us.

King might reiterate that the song-writer answered the prophet Jeremiah's questions, "Is there no balm in Gilead? Is there no physician there?" (Jeremiah 8:22) with an affirmation of faith punctuated with an exclamation point:

There is a balm in Gilead... to make the wounded whole...

There is a balm in Gilead... to heal the sin-sick soul...

Sometimes I feel discouraged...

And think my work's in vain...

But then the Holy Spirt revives my soul again!

Some good news in the midst of waiting can be found in that David's fifteen-chapter, long-playing album about waiting turned into a song of praise and answered prayer in Psalm 40. David, at the end of his mixtape, sang about what the Lord did while he waited, "*I waited patiently for the Lord; God turned to me and heard my cry. God lifted me out of the slimy pit, out of the mud and mire; God set my feet on a rock and gave me a firm place to stand. God put a new song in my mouth, a hymn of praise to our God*" (vv. 1-3).

The evidence shows that if we wait on the Lord, God might not come when we want God to come, *but God will show up.* The evidence shows that if we keep looking up with faith and hope, *God is going to show up.* The evidence shows that *God is an on-time God.* The evidence shows that as we wait, God will put a new song in our mouths, *a hymn of praise to our God.* And the evidence shows that as we wait on the Lord, it is always darkest just before daybreak.

Indeed, as David would exclaim in the middle of his fifteen-chapter mixtape, in Psalm 30:5, "*Weeping may endure for a night, but joy comes in the morning!*"

This *fierce urgency of now* – the sense of urgency that is ours - tells us that we must not give up on God or each other. It tells us that the same God who blessed us before will bless us again. And it tells us that we must live fully and faithfully in this very moment as we wait on the Lord. The sentiments of the great theologian Benjamin Elijah Mays ring true for us in this urgent moment of history –

> *I've only just a minute,*
> *With sixty seconds in it,*
> *Forced upon me, can't refuse it,*
> *Didn't seek it, didn't choose it.*

But it's up to me to use it,
I must suffer if I lose it,
Give account if I abuse it.
Just a tiny little minute,
But eternity is in it.

5 - *A FIERCE URGENCY OF NOW (An Essay)*

(This address was given at the Ebony Scholarship Society's 25th Annual Martin Luther King, Jr. Breakfast, New Carrollton, MD, Monday, January 21, 2019)

"But wanting to justify himself, he asked Jesus, "And who is my neighbor?"   *(Luke 10:29; 25-37)*

This year marks the 90th anniversary of Rev. Dr. Martin Luther King, Jr.'s birth, and the 51st year after his assassination on April 4, 1968 in Memphis, TN. As was the case in 1968, the nation and world today are fraught with social, economic, political and religious upheaval. Over the past several years, we have become more divided along various lines. In the U.S., the social and political division that we now experience is not really new, but it challenges our sense of normalcy in ways that perhaps we have not been challenged in the past.

Indeed, much progress was eventuated in America up to King's assassination on a balcony at the Lorraine Motel in Memphis at 6:01 pm on April 4, 1968. This progress was seen in the passing of national Civil Rights and Voting Rights legislation in the mid-1960's, and this progress seemed to come to full fruition with the election of Barack H. Obama in 2008 as the 44th President of the United States, the first African American to hold the nation's highest office.

And yet, subsequent years have seen the heightened emergence (or re-emergence) of evils such as racism, classism, sexism, misogyny, homophobia, Islamophobia, anti-immigration, war and terror (to name some) that have served to divide much of society, and even large segments of the churches.

On August 28, 1963, on the steps of the Lincoln Memorial, in Washington, DC, gospel singer Mahalia Jackson, encouraged King to "Tell them about the Dream, Martin!" And most us, and much of the world are familiar with the dream that he proceeded to share. In his speech on that sunlit day in the Nation's Capital, in the concluding recitation in what has come to be known as the "I Have a Dream" speech, King described to the world his dream of the *Beloved Community,* when girls and boys of all races could play together and go to school together, and where people would be judged by the content of their character, and not the color of their skin.

What is often lost amidst the eloquent words of his "I Have a Dream" recitation at the end of his remarks that day is that earlier in the speech King spoke of something equally as important to those who heard it then, and to us who hear it today. He spoke of *"the fierce urgency of now,"* the need for immediate, "vigorous and positive action" in overcoming racism and other "isms" in our society.

He said, *"We are now faced with the fact that tomorrow is today. We are confronted with the fierce urgency of now. In this unfolding conundrum of life and history, there "is" such a thing as being too late. This is no time for apathy or complacency. This is a time for vigorous and positive action."*

26

Earlier in 1963 in Detroit, Michigan, King had similarly alluded to this urgency. He said *"But these events that are taking place in our nation tell us something else. They tell us that the Negro and his allies in the white community now recognize the urgency of the moment... And so, this social revolution taking place can be summarized in three little words. They are not big words. One does not need an extensive vocabulary to understand them. They are the words "all," "here," and "now." We want all of our rights, we want them here, and we want them now."*

And so, today, we might wonder what King might say to the church and society in light of where we find ourselves, and in light of what he had to say about the *fierce urgency of now* some 56 years ago. To paint a picture of where society found itself during his lifetime, in 1968, King shared the story of the Good Samaritan, and offered a depiction of the Jericho road (Luke 10:25-37). He said, that the "Jericho road is a dangerous road ... It's a winding, meandering road."

But wanting to justify himself, the Pharisee asked Jesus, "And who is my neighbor?" (Luke 10:29)

If King were here today, he might remind us that the Samaritan offered creatively altruistic concern to his neighbor, and then he might offer insight on what it means to show such altruistic concern on the various "Jericho roads" that we must now travel today. *He might remind us that the creative altruism that the Good Samaritan demonstrated was universal, excessive and dangerous.*

Through this parable, Jesus disclosed his definition of a neighbor. A neighbor is Jew and Gentile; she/he is Russian and American; he/she is Muslim and Christian; she/he is

Native American, Hispanic and Asian, white and black. She/he is richer and poorer – left and right – conservative and liberal – Democratic, Republican and Independent. A neighbor is "any certain man or woman" – any person in need – on any of the numerous Jericho roads of life.

King might further remind us that today, the most important expression of this type of *universal, excessive and dangerous* altruism is seen in *how we raise our children, and work to secure their future. Why is this important?*

Dr. Marion Wright Edelman, of the Children's Defense Fund, states:

We are at risk of letting our children drown in the bathwater of American materialism, greed and violence. We must regain our spiritual bearings and roots, and help America recover hers before millions more children – Black, Brown and white, poor, middle-class and rich – self-destruct or grow up thinking life is about acquiring rather than sharing, selfishness rather than sacrifice, and material rather than spiritual wealth. And even as so much progress has been made, for too many Black children and families, progress is not coming quickly enough or at all.[1]

Consider these recent statistics about black children living in the U.S.:

- Every five seconds during the school day, a Black public-school student is suspended.

---

[1] Robert Franklin, *Crisis in the Village: Restoring Hope in African American Communities* (Minneapolis: Fortress Press, 2007), p 20.

- Every forty-six seconds during the school day, a Black high school student drops out.
- Every minute, a Black child is arrested and a Black baby is born to an unmarried mother.
- Every three minutes, a Black child is born into poverty.
- Every hour, a Black baby dies.
- Every four, hours a Black child or youth under twenty dies from an accident.
- Every five hours, a Black child or youth under twenty is a homicide victim.
- Every day, a Black young person under twenty-five dies from HIV infection.
- Every day, a Black child or youth under twenty commits suicide.

Edelman goes on to state that we must learn to reweave the rich fabric of community for our children and to re-install the values and sense of purpose our elders and mentors have always embraced... A massive new movement must well up from every nook, cranny, and place in our community involving millions of parents; religious, civic, educational, business, and political leaders; and youths themselves.[2]

And what more might King want us to be mindful of as it regards the *fierce urgency of now*?

If King were here, *he might also remind us about the fundamental nature of humanity*, and that we have all been created by the same God, and that God loves all of that which

---

[2] Franklin., 21.

has been divinely created. Thus, there is a reminder of the *inherent worth, and human dignity in each of us, and what King referred to as the "somebodyness" of all of humanity.*

Thus, the reminder today as King stated that *"We are caught in an inescapable network of mutuality, tied in a single garment of destiny. Whatever affects one directly, affects all indirectly."*

If King were here with us, *he might then remind us that ours is to be a constant striving for peace with justice.* He intimated that *"true peace is not merely the absence of tension; it is the presence of justice".* Thus, ours must be a continuous yearning for peace with justice. *It is not expedient or sufficient in this day and age for any of us to just go along to get along.*

He might then remind us that the work for righteousness, justice and peace is not to be confined to any one group of people. The work for righteousness, justice and peace is not merely the work of Blacks or Whites, Christians, Jews or Muslims, left or right, conservatives or liberals, or any other particular group - *but the work for righteousness and justice belongs to each and every one of us.*

The sentiments of King's friend, Rabbi Abraham Joshua Heschel resonate, *"Morally speaking, there is no limit to the concern one must feel for the suffering of human beings; indifference to evil is worse than evil itself, and in a free society, some are guilty, but all are responsible."*

Finally, if King were here with us today, he might end with reminding us that with whatever circumstances we face as the church and society, *we must never give up hoping.* According to King, *"Hope is the refusal to give up despite overwhelming odds."* For him, hope was to be viewed as *"animated and undergirded by faith and love."* So, no matter what, keep hoping.

He might move to conclude by urging us not to forget his words on the steps of the Lincoln Memorial in August 1963 in the dream that he shared with the nation that there would someday be *"hewn out of the mountain of despair, a stone of hope."*

And perhaps he would close by reminding us of the words of a song made famous by his friend Ms. Mahalia Jackson, that might be our anthem today:

If I can help somebody as I travel along,
If I can cheer somebody with a word or a song,
If I can help somebody as they're living wrong,
Then my living will not be in vain...

If I can do my duty, as a Christian ought,
If I can bring back beauty, to a world up wrought,
If I can spread love's message, as the Master taught
Then my living will not be in vain.

6 - *WHEN DREAMS ARE DESTROYED*
(A Sermon)

Joseph had a dream, and when he told it to his brothers, they hated him all the more. He said to them, "Listen to this dream I had: We were binding sheaves of grain out in the field when suddenly my sheaf rose and stood upright, while your sheaves gathered around mine and bowed down to it." His brothers said to him, "Do you intend to reign over us? Will you actually rule us?" And they hated him all the more because of his dream and what he had said. Then he had another dream, and he told it to his brothers. "Listen," he said, "I had another dream, and this time the sun and moon and eleven stars were bowing down to me." When he told his father as well as his brothers, his father rebuked him and said, "What is this dream you had? Will your mother and I and your brothers actually come and bow down to the ground before you?" His brothers were jealous of him, but his father kept the matter in mind. (Genesis 37:5-11)

Dreams have a certain allure for us because they often conjure thoughts, offer images, and stoke our imagination of things that we may yearn for in our lives and in the lives of others. I'd venture to suggest that all of us have dreamt at some point, and at other times, have been beneficiaries of somebody's dreams for us. Many parents dream of a better future for their children than has been their own fate in life. I do believe that I'm the beneficiary of the dreams of others. I'm living on the dreams of my parents and grandparents, and their parents. And I know I'm not alone.

Indeed, dreams can be powerful. This year (2018) we've observed the 89th year of the birth and 50th year of the assassination of the greatest American dreamer, Rev. Dr. Martin Luther King, Jr., who on August 28, 1963 on the steps of the Lincoln Memorial in Washington, DC, at the urging of Ms. Mahalia Jackson, shared with the world his dream.

King's was a dream where his children could play with, and go to school with children of all races. He dreamt a world where we would all be judged by the content of our character, and not the color of our skin.

In the book of Genesis, we find that Joseph was likewise a dreamer. Like many dreams, his pointed to the prospect of change and supernatural possibility that could only be effected by God.

But Joseph's story, like King's, *shows us that daring to dream can cost us.* Joseph's dream frightened his brothers who decided that they would kill Joseph and his dream, and later his dreaming would concern even his father, Jacob.

Indeed, if we dare to dream, *we might face some dream-killers.* Our dreams can cost us. *Something that we find with Joseph's dream was that it was only really understood and recognized by Joseph.* His brothers derided him for it, maybe because they didn't think his dreams were real.

When God gives you a dream, don't be surprised if you and God are the only two who recognize it. And don't be surprised if other people, even those close to you, don't fully understand the dream that God has placed before you to see.

King realized that many people didn't understand his dream years after he shared it with the world. In 1967, he shared about how his dream had become a nightmare. *"I must confess that that dream that I had that day has in many points turned into a nightmare. Now I'm not one to lose hope. I keep on hoping. I still have faith in the future. But I've had to analyze many things over the last few years and I would say over the last few months."*

If the truth is really told today, many of us can relate - 50 years later - with how King sensed that his dream had become a nightmare.

We live in the midst of shattered dreams, today. Shattered dreams of justice, shattered dreams of peace... shattered dreams of love... shattered dreams of harmony... shattered dreams of nobody being hungry... shattered dreams of no woman being assaulted... and shattered dreams of no child being left behind.

Joseph faced the prospect of his dreams being shattered by the bitterness and backstabbing of his own brothers. *His brothers hated him for the favor on his life, and hated him even more when he had the nerve to dream.*

But in the midst of hate and evil, in the midst of the conniving and contriving of his brothers, Joseph kept the faith, and kept believing that the same God who gave him the dream, would bring his dream to fruition. The great American poet, Langston Hughes was a dreamer like Joseph. Hughes dreamt a world-:

> *... where man*
> *No other man will scorn,*
> *Where love will bless the earth*
> *And peace its paths adorn*
> *... a world where all*
> *Will know sweet freedom's way,*

Where greed no longer saps the soul,
Nor avarice blights our day.
A world… where black or white,
Whatever race you be,
Will share the bounties of the earth,
　　And every man is free.

What is God's dream for your life? How is God daring you to dream? Whatever your dream is, just hold to it.

Even when our dreams seem to be destroyed, might we muster the temerity to heed again the sentiments of Langston Hughes –

Hold fast to dreams
For if dreams die
Life is a broken-winged bird
That cannot fly.

Hold fast to dreams
For when dreams go
Life is a barren field
Frozen with snow.

7 - A PRAYER FOR THE NEW YEAR
(By Howard Thurman)

God,
Grant that I may pass through the coming year with a faithful heart. There will be much to test me and make weak my strength before the year ends.

In my confusion I shall often say the word that is not true and do the thing of which I am ashamed. There will be errors in the mind and great inaccuracies of judgment.

In seeking the light,
I shall again and again find myself
walking in the darkness.

I shall mistake my light for Your light
and I shall drink from the responsibility of the choice I make.

Though my days be marked with failures, stumblings, fallings, let my spirit be free so that You may take it and redeem my moments in all the ways my needs reveal.

Give me the quiet assurance of Your Love and Presence. Grant that I may pass through the coming year with a faithful heart.

8 - A RIGHT-POSITIONED HOPE (A Sermon)

I said, "I will watch my ways and keep my tongue from sin; I will put a muzzle on my mouth while in the presence of the wicked." So, I remained utterly silent, not even saying anything good. But my anguish increased; my heart grew hot within me. While I meditated, the fire burned; then I spoke with my tongue: "Show me, Lord, my life's end and the number of my days; let me know how fleeting my life is. You have made my days a mere handbreadth; the span of my years is as nothing before you. Everyone is but a breath, even those who seem secure. "Surely everyone goes around like a mere phantom; in vain they rush about, heaping up wealth without knowing whose it will finally be. But now, Lord, what do I look for? My hope is in you. (Psalm 39:1-7)

Sickness and sorrow, sadness and suffering - these are things that can burden us to the point of *unbelieving thoughts*, and even *faithlessness.* If we are truthful, these things may lead us to the inability to pray, and lead us out of proximity with God. It really doesn't matter who we are, from where we've come, where we've gone to school, where we live, how much money we may or may not have in the bank - storms of life can and will come into our lives, disturb us, mess us up, and turn life topsy-turvy.

Perennial questions in times like these are, "Where is God in the midst of our going through? What is the efficacy and effectuality of our faith?" "Where might we find hope?"

This was the place and predicament of the psalmist in Psalm 39. This is a song of David who was coming to the end of his life, and reflecting on the meaning of all that he had gone through. It is, in many ways, a blues song, a sorrow song like our ancestors would sing in centuries past, *"Nobody knows the trouble I've seen…"*

In Psalm 38, the psalmist looked back over his life and wrote about being sick, *"Because of your wrath there is no health in my body; there is no soundness in my bones because of my sin." (Psalm 38:3)*

And here in Psalm 39, in part-two of this song, David is looking at the prospect of his final days. *"Show me, Lord, my life's end and the number of my days; let me know how fleeting my life is."* (v. 4)

David's reckoning with his human frailty and finitude can help us who are going through any form of difficulty today, and help us with what we might go through tomorrow. David was like you, me, and everybody else who is trying to walk by faith and not by sight. He was like everybody else who is trying to find hope in the midst of existential darkness.

He had been faithful, he had been prayerful, he had been full of worship and praise, and he loved God with his whole heart. But David now found himself facing the realities of life and death, of going through. And not just going through, but he was going through to the point of wanting to give up on God, and on life.

If we pay close attention, we can feel David's pain. We can empathize with David. What's the use of faith for mothers and fathers separated from their children at America's borders? What's the use of faith for the 348 families whose loved ones were murdered in Baltimore city in 2019, or for the 50 families who lost loved ones to murder in Baltimore County in 2019?

What good is faith for persons who slept on grates last night, and those who will have nothing to eat today? What good is faith for those who are sick, and have no healthcare?

David's predicament is a reminder for us that we might get to the place in life where we wonder "what's the use?" Life deals us blow after blow, difficulty after difficulty, trial after trial, and we might be led to ask, "What's the use?" Troubles and tribulations come, valleys and vicissitudes meet us, despair and disappointments greet us, and we wonder, "Why?" Where is God in the midst of it all?" "What's the use?"

Indeed, David's song reminds us that there could be junctures in life where we realize that our faith does not make us immune to suffering. There might be points at which the songs that have encouraged us before, won't suffice, and sermons won't get us through.

So, what then will help us? What do we, as people of faith, have at our disposal?

What we have at our disposal is hope. David concluded Psalm 39 by helping us to know that *at the end of it all, with everything we've gone through and may go through, we have a right-positioned hope.* He shares an affirmation of his faith in the living God. *"But now, Lord, what do I look for? My hope is in you."* (v. 7)

Dr. Martin Luther King, Jr. said in a 1967 sermon, "The Meaning of Hope", that *"Hope is the refusal to give up despite insurmountable odds."* Dr. Walter Brueggemann in his book a *Gospel of Hope* writes that *"Hope is the deep religious conviction that God has not quit."*

Concerning hope, St. Augustine the fourth century Bishop of Hippo said that *"Hope has two beautiful daughters; their names are Anger and Courage. Anger at the way things are, and Courage to see that they do not remain as they are."* Hope does not settle for the status quo.

King further stated that hope is always animated by our faith and love, and that if we have hope, we have faith in something.

David said, *"But now, Lord, what do I look for? My hope is in you."* We learn from David that at the end of it all, when it's all said and done, we can rest assured when our hope is in the Lord. Indeed, what we as people of faith have in our spiritual arsenal is hope (if we don't have anything else). Why? Because, regardless of how bad things are or how difficult days may become - God has not quit. Hope says that God is not dead and God is not done!

Ours is a right-positioned hope. Such hope assures us that *"weeping may endure for a night, but joy comes in the morning." (Psalm 30:5)*

What does a right-positioned hope look like?

> *Hope reminds us that God is not finished with any of us yet.*
> *Hope insists that greater is God who is in us, than he who is in the world.*
> *Hope says that we can do all things through Christ who strengthens us.*
> *Hope helps us to know that we may not know what tomorrow holds, but we know who holds tomorrow.*
> *Hope woke us up this morning.*
> *Hope started us on our way.*

Hope put food on the table... clothes on our backs.
Hope clothed us in our right minds.
Hope healed the sick.
Hope raised the dead.
Hope took two fish and five loaves of bread,
and fed more than five thousand hungry people.
Hope deliverers, saves, and redeems us.

Our hope is in the Lord! A right-positioned hope is a hope that's alive. It's a hope that's not dead, dormant, drab, dreary, dull, latent, stagnant, stale or vapid. A right-positioned hope beckons us to keep dreaming with an animated faith. Ours is a right-positioned hope, and might we hold to the lyrics of the great hymn –

My hope is built on nothing less
Than Jesus' blood and righteousness.
I dare not trust the sweetest frame
But wholly lean in Jesus's name.
On Christ the solid Rock I stand
All other ground is sinking sand.

9 - THE COURAGE TO BE COMMUNITY (An Essay)

(This message was delivered at Mercy Medical Center, Baltimore, Maryland, Monday, January 20, 2020 for the annual commemoration of Rev. Dr. Martin Luther King, Jr.'s birthday.)

This year marks the 91st anniversary of Rev. Dr. Martin Luther King, Jr.'s birth, and the 52nd year after his assassination on April 4, 1968 in Memphis, TN. As was the case in 1968, the nation and world today are fraught with social, economic, political and religious upheaval. Over the past several years, we have become more divided along various lines. In the U.S., the social and political division that we now experience is not really new, but it challenges our sense of normalcy and community in ways that perhaps we have not been challenged in the past.

King's singular vision was for the realization of the *Beloved Community*. In their seminal 1974 work entitled, *Search for the Beloved Community,* Kenneth Smith and Ira Zepp, Jr. suggested that King's perspective on the Christian love-ethic provides critical insight into understanding his persistent search for the *Beloved Community*. For him, *the Beloved Community* was rooted in the biblical notion of *agape* (God's unconditional love), and was the ultimate goal for society.[3]

---

[3] Kenneth Smith and Ira Zepp, Jr., *Search for the Beloved Community: The Thinking of Martin Luther King, Jr.,* (Valley Forge, PA: Judson Press, 1974, 1998), see pp. 129-156.

With regard to courage, and the courage to be community, interestingly, among the books that King constantly carried with him as he travelled and provided leadership with the Civil Rights movement over a 14-year period, was Paul Tillich's *The Courage to Be.*

Concerning courage, Tillich wrote, "Few constructs are as useful for analysis of the human situation. Courage is an ethical reality, but it is rooted in the whole breadth of human existence and ultimately in the structure of being, itself. It must be considered ontologically in order to be understood ethically."[4]

King's courage was born and bred out of the needs of the times in which he was called forth to provide prophetic voice and leadership. His courage was similar to that which Queen Esther was summoned to in being an agent of protection and deliverance for her people. Amidst her perilous plight, and discerning if and how to act, her cousin Mordecai reminded her, *"Who knows—perhaps it was for a time like this that you became queen?"* (Esther 4:14)

For King, it was such courage that would result in the refusal to give up against the insurmountable odds of racism and class oppression. He stated in *Where do We Go from Here?* that "This refusal to stop, this "courage to be", this determination to go on "in spite of" is the hallmark of any great movement."[5]

---

[4] Paul Tillich, *The Courage to Be* (New Haven: Yale University Press, 1952), 1.
[5] Martin Luther King, Jr., *Where Do We Go from Here: Chaos or Community?* (Boston: Beacon Press, 2010) pp. 54-55.

And so, as it regards the courage to be community now into the 21st century, what might King remind us of today?

King might remind us that in his conception of the *Beloved Community*, faith and action were interrelated. In this regard, theology and ethics were inextricably connected. Theology – what we believe and comprehend about God (how we talk about God) can not be separated from ethics – how we behave as the human family. Our creed and our deed have to be in concert. Our talk and our walk have to correspond. Our faith and action have to correlate.

This faith-action (creed-deed) dialectic found its ultimate expression in the notion of the *Beloved Community*. For King, there were two steps involved in the movement toward the *Beloved Community*. First, *desegregation* would lead to the removal of legal barriers to equality. But *desegregation* was a short-term goal – and it alone was not enough. Desegregation had to be followed by *integration*. *Integration* advocated and facilitated the inclusion of all persons in a just society. King defined *integration* as genuine inter-group, interpersonal living. *Integration* was the long-term goal as a means toward realizing the vision of *Beloved Community*.

King asserted that "all life is interrelated." One of his fundamental beliefs was in the kinship of all persons. He believed all life is part of a single process; all living things are interrelated; and all persons are sisters and brothers. All have a place in the *Beloved Community*. Because all are interrelated, one cannot harm another without harming oneself. King said, "To the degree that I harm my brother, no matter what he is doing to me, to that extent I am harming myself. For example, white men often refuse federal aid to education in order to avoid giving the Negro his rights; but because all men are brothers, they cannot deny Negro children without harming themselves."[6]

King might also remind us that community always beckons us to reconciliation. When the Montgomery Bus Boycott ended, he spoke at a victory rally on December 3, 1956. He spoke words of hope for the future, and pointed out that the goal of the boycott had not been to defeat other persons, but to awaken the conscience of others to challenge the false sense of superiority that persons might harbor. Now that victory had been achieved, King said, it was time for reconciliation. "The end is reconciliation; the end is the creation of *Beloved Community*."

He might remind us that the *Beloved Community* is to be an integrated community in which persons of all races and creeds live together harmoniously as sisters and brothers in peace. It is the kin-dom of God on earth. King stated, "I do not think of political power as an end. Neither do I think of economic power as an end. They are ingredients in the objective we seek in life. And I think that end, that objective, is a truly brotherly society, the creation of *Beloved Community*."[7]

Finally, I don't think King would stop without reminding us that courage is a main ingredient of hope. St. Augustine of Hippo intimated that *"Hope has two beautiful*

---

[6] Martin Luther King, Jr., "Loving Your Enemies," *Strength to Love* (New York: York: Harper, 1963), pp. 41-50.

[7] Martin Luther King, Jr., "Suffering and Faith" in *The Christian Century* (Chicago, IL: Christian Century, July 13, 1966).

daughters; their names are Anger and Courage. Anger at the way things are, and Courage to see that they do not remain as they are." Thus, in striving to be community, *we must never give up hoping.* According to King, *"Hope is the refusal to give up despite overwhelming odds."* For him, hope was to be viewed as *"animated and undergirded by faith and love."* So, no matter what, keep hoping.

10 - WHAT HAVE WE WROUGHT?
– THE LEGACY OF THE WASHINGTON CONFERENCE
(An Essay)

(This article was published in the United Methodist Connection of the United Methodist Church, Fulton, MD in 2014)

Growing up in the Methodist Church, it often puzzled me as to why and how there came to be so many Methodist Churches located in such close proximity to one another. St. Paul Methodist Church in Oxon Hill, Maryland – the church in which I was baptized as an infant, and in which I was a member through my youth – was a small church, all of whose members were black. Although I was regularly taken to church by my parents and grandparents, the problem of race in the church really didn't dawn on me until 1969 when I was eight years old.

That was the year that St. Paul received its first white minister. That was also the year that there began to be discussions and outward overtures from the white Methodist church around the corner (Oxon Hill Methodist Church) about shared ministries and possible merger. Up to that point, the two churches seemed to exist in two separate worlds. Although they were less than a mile apart, in the same denomination, and supposedly worshipping and serving the same God, the churches were in fact essentially invisible to each other.

It was at the point when serious talks of shared ministry and merger began that the realities of racial division in the church came to the surface for the members of both St. Paul and Oxon Hill churches. Up until 1968, St. Paul, one of the oldest Methodist churches in Maryland, had been a part of the Washington Conference and the Central Jurisdiction - all-black, segregated sub-structures that had been created within the larger, majority white Methodist denomination, with the uniting of Methodist factions in 1939, while Oxon Hill had been an established and well-regarded member of the Baltimore Conference and the broader Methodist Church.

The creation of the United Methodist Church in 1968, with the merger of the Evangelical United Brethren Churches in Christ and the Methodist Church, and the subsequent elimination of the Central Jurisdiction - and effectively the Washington Conference - offered what seemed to be new hope that local congregations like St. Paul and Oxon Hill, which had up to that point remained segregated, could heal their racial wounds and work toward reconciliation and eventual union.

Despite the hope engendered by these circumstances, the talk of congregational merger brought the often-unspoken historical wounds of race division painfully to the fore. Who would be the pastor of a newly merged racially integrated congregation? Would she or he be black or white? How would the committees of the new church be established? How would power and leadership be shared in the congregation? How would finances and property be handled? Who would "own" the property of the newly merged congregation? In what style would the new congregation worship? The talks of merger eventually ceased, and today these two congregations continue to co-exist less than a mile apart from one another.

The experiences of St. Paul and Oxon Hill United Methodist Churches are not unique within the historical context of Methodism.

In October, we will celebrate the 150th anniversary of slave emancipation in Maryland and the creation of the Washington Conference in Methodism. Bishop James Thomas intimates in the title of his book on the story of the Central Jurisdiction that its existence was Methodism's "racial dilemma." *(Methodism's Racial Dilemma: The Story of the Central Jurisdiction)* At the meeting at which the Washington Conference was formally established as a part of the Central Jurisdiction, it has been said that Bishop Edgar Love asked, "What have we wrought?" For black Methodists, the results of the "Uniting Conference of 1939" in Kansas City and the establishment of the Central Jurisdiction (and subsequently the Washington Conference) effectively meant the establishment of a "denomination within a denomination – a segregated church within a church."

What have we wrought? Rev. Dr. William B. McLain, in his 1999 article entitled, "When a Dream is Deferred," intimates that the creation of the Central Jurisdiction was yet another effort of the Methodist Church to rid itself of the race problem by sweeping it under the church's "rug", as was evident with the 1939 Plan of Union and the compromises among the Methodist Episcopal Church, the Methodist Episcopal Church South and the Methodist Protestant Church. One of the selling points of the establishment of an all-black jurisdiction and conferences was that black Methodists would be allowed to elect their own bishops and build their own institutions.

In 1968, at the dawn of the formation of the United Methodist Church and the elimination of the former Central Jurisdiction, Dr. Martin Luther King, Jr. eloquently and prophetically cautioned that with the elimination of the Central Jurisdiction, there existed the possibility of black Methodists "being integrated out of power." Some forty-six years later we are left to ponder the profundity and acuity of King's observation. McClain asserted that notwithstanding the 1968 merger, the legacy of segregation has continued to plague the United Methodist Church.

What have we wrought? Indeed, the effects of church segregation of the past persist in United Methodism today. In fact, the vast majority of United Methodist congregations – across racial, ethnic and geographic lines - remain essentially segregated. The United Methodist Church remains largely segregated with over 90 percent of its members in the United States being white (Pew Research Center). The legacy of racial segregation is most evident in the decline of many black United Methodist congregations. Over the past fifty years - this decline is apparent in consistently decreasing membership, worship attendance, stewardship, and diminished vitality in worship and witness in many churches.

And yet today, a biblical-theological prospect, as rooted in a question raised by the prophet Ezekiel in the 6th century B.C.E., is before us. "Who will stand in the breach? I looked for anyone among them who would repair the wall and stand in the breach...but I found no one." (Ez. 22:30) As one who is counted among those who are products of the Washington Conference, and as a committed United Methodist, I stand with many others on the legacy of our segregated past with a hope rooted in the promises of God of a unified and fully empowered people. As we who are of many hues continue to work together towards truly becoming the "United" Methodist Church, this is a hope that with God's help, our future will outshine our tragic past.

11- HOPE BORN OUT OF HISTORY: TELLING THE WHOLE TRUTH *(An Essay)*

(This is the manuscript of a video presentation for the "Who are We?" study series of the Baltimore-Washington Conference of the United Methodist Church, January, 2019)

Who are we? This is essentially a question of identity for us as people who are United Methodist. It is a question that relates to our past, places us in our present, and points us to our future. As United Methodists, people of Wesleyan faith traditions, we have been a diverse people from our origins. At the historic Christmas Conference in 1784, persons of diverse backgrounds gathered at Lovely Lane Chapel in Baltimore to covenant together and shape a vision of what Methodism – the Wesleyan movement - would look like in America.

Among those in attendance were at least two African Americans – Richard Allen, and Harry Hoosier, with Allen and Absalom Jones being the first African Americans to receive license to preach by the newly formed Methodist Episcopal Church in 1785.

Notes from the African American Methodist Heritage Center point to the racial diversity incumbent across the history of American Methodism: "The history, heritage and hopes of United Methodists of African descent are inextricably intertwined with the history, heritage, and hopes of John Wesley's Methodism since its beginnings in North America. Yet the whole church has been slow to celebrate that linkage, perhaps due to a lack of knowledge and understanding of the story, trials and triumphs."

Indeed, the challenges in living into our racial diversity (as well as other forms of diversity) have been formidable. The 1844 split of Methodism into Northern and Southern denominations was effectively an outcome of the debate over slavery and segregation imbedded in churches - at local levels through early denominational structures – with most notable cases being the experience of African American worshippers at St. George's Church in Philadelphia and Johns Street Church in New York City, where Black worshippers were effectively forced to leave their churches due to segregationist ecclesial practices.

The 1939 Methodist Unity Conference in Kansas City, Missouri, served to create the segregated, all-Black Central Jurisdiction. And although the 1968 establishment of the United Methodist Church effectively disestablished the Central Jurisdiction and legally abolished structural racism in American Methodism, the remnants of racial segregation, and other forms of struggles to live into our diversity, remain today.

Today, the latest Pew Research Center data shows that the United Methodist Church in America is about 94 percent white, with Blacks (including African Americans), Latinx, Asians and Native Americans together comprising the remaining 6 percent of American United Methodists. The racial-ethnic diversity of United Methodism in America does not reflect the growing diversity across the country in general, where over 37 percent of Americans are now non-white persons.

A part of our biblical and theological imperative has been and continues to be to ask the question, "should the church be divided by race, age, gender and socio-economic status? Most people would clearly say 'no'. We could point to the apostle Paul's assertion in Galatians 3:26-29 that:

> *For in Christ Jesus you are all children of God through faith. As many of you as were baptized into Christ have clothed yourselves with Christ. There is no longer Jew or Greek, there is no longer slave or free, there is no longer male and female; for all of you are one in Christ Jesus. And if you belong to Christ, then you are Abraham's offspring, heirs according to the promise.*

Furthermore, we might see God's will and desire for the church and the world as evidenced in the words of the psalmist in Psalm 133:1-3:

> *How very good and pleasant it is when kindred live together in unity! It is like the precious oil on the head, running down upon the beard, on the beard of Aaron, running down over the collar of his robes. It is like the dew of Hermon, which falls on the mountains of Zion. For there the Lord ordained God's blessing, life forevermore.*

It is clear that race continues to matter in America, and that we are not yet at the place of being post-racial or post-racist in the churches or society. Michael Eric Dyson addressed this matter in his book, *Can You Hear Me Now?*, where he insists that the critical question that is before us today is not if we are yet a *post-racial* society, and the question is not even if we should strive to become post-racial, but the critical question is how might we move closer towards becoming a *post-racist* society? The same question is before the church. How might we move closer to becoming a *post-racist* church?

The path toward healing the wounds of racism and other forms of division in the Methodist family can begin with finding ways of acknowledging and learning from our past, and building upon the work has been done to get us to where we are.

In the Baltimore-Washington Conference, we can learn from many examples, including:

- Asbury Church in DC, an historically Black, still vital congregation that was founded out of Foundry Church
- Mt. Zion Church in DC, another historically Black, still vital congregation founded out of Dumbarton Church
- Wesley Freedom Church in Carroll County, MD and their story of opposing slavery, and where slave owners were turned away from their congregation
- Epworth Chapel in Baltimore, a vital inner suburban church in a racially, economically and socially diverse and transitioning community, where persons from over 15 nations are now a part of the regular worshipping congregation
- Waters and Brooks Churches in southern Maryland – two churches – one predominantly white and the other

predominantly black, which continue to come to grips with the legacy of race and racism in their churches and community.

And so, how is the church today being called to redemption, reconciliation and transformation? How do we combat the remnants of the sin of segregation? Where there is division in any form among us, there must be authentic redemption and reconciliation before there can be spiritual and social transformation. The following four areas might lead to further discernment in addressing these two questions.

1. *Acknowledgement and Affirmation* – How do we acknowledge and affirm our common creation by God? How do we then acknowledge and affirm the full humanity of all people? In light of it, how do we acknowledge and affirm the past and present wounds of racism and other "isms", name them, then commit to proactively seeking to build community across difference?

2. *Authenticity and Association* – In what ways, as individuals and churches, might we commit to engaging and embracing difference? How might we strive to build community based on principles of authenticity and sincerity, and substantive, sustained levels of human association across difference?

3. *Articulation and Aspiration* – What are the individual and collective experiences, narratives, stories, images and metaphors that have shaped our worldview and understanding of community? How might these be articulated in ways that inform the present, and point to the future.

4. *Anticipation and Appropriation* – What future do we anticipate, and what hopes and dreams do we have for a better future when it comes to overcoming racism and other forms of segregation? In what ways can our hopes and dreams be appropriated into a future that is even more inclusive and diverse than our past and present?

12 - WHERE DO WE GO FROM HERE? FULL INCLUSION, DIVISION OR WHAT? *(An Essay)*

(This article was published in the United Methodist Connection of the United Methodist Church, Fulton, MD in June 2017)

I am a fifth generation Methodist. I was baptized, confirmed and nurtured in the Christian faith at St. Paul United Methodist Church in Oxon Hill, MD and Gibbons United Methodist Church in Brandywine, MD. I sensed God's calling on my life to offer myself in service to the church in the ordained ministry as a young adult at Gibbons Church.

I am a United Methodist by birth and by choice. I was born into Methodism, and I remain a Methodist because the Methodist church and Wesleyan experiences of faith and grace have been where God has been most extant and real for me - places of invitation, welcome and radical hospitality.

In many of the places that I have travelled and served in ministry over the years, I have experienced the face of God through such radical hospitality. I have experienced the rich diversity of the church while serving as a district superintendent of two diverse districts, as a denominational executive serving across the diverse expanse of the Northeastern Jurisdiction, the United States and the world, and as a seminary professor where all of the places I have taught have been culturally diverse, and diverse in other ways. I have served as a pastor of churches that have been culturally diverse, and diverse in other ways. The congregation that I now serve, Epworth Chapel United Methodist Church in Baltimore, MD, is blessed with persons who were born in at least 15 different nations, and is diverse in other ways as well. I am also blessed to serve as the chairperson of the Baltimore-Washington Conference Board of Ordained Ministry, a group of sixty person who are culturally diverse, and diverse in other ways.

I choose to remain a United Methodist as an African-American, and I am fully cognizant of the fact that racial segregation persisted in the American Methodist church's structures for over 100 years. I am cognizant that the church practiced discrimination against women for over 170 years by denying women the opportunity to serve as fully ordained ministers in the life of the Church.

Today, in the Baltimore-Washington Conference, many people in our local churches, like our denomination and our society, are not of the same mind on a number of important matters that affect persons who are a part of us, including on matters pertaining to the full inclusion of LGBTQI+ persons in the life of the Church.

At the 2017 Baltimore-Washington Annual Conference Clergy Executive session, one of our colleagues, Rev. Dr. Phillip Wogaman, decided to surrender his clergy credentials in protest of the United Methodist Church's current stance prohibiting the full inclusion of LGBTQI+ persons in the life of the Church, and in protest of the Baltimore-Washington Conference Board of Ordained Ministry's decision to delay a prior decision to recommend one of its candidates for commissioning as a provisional clergy member.

I am among those who grieve Wogaman's decision to relinquish his clergy credentials. I have known him since my time as a student at Wesley Theological Seminary where he was then the academic dean, and throughout my entire 25-year career as a pastor in the Baltimore-Washington Conference. One of the highlights of my ministry was having the opportunity to sit together and engage in Holy Conferencing with Wogaman during the entire 2008 Northeastern Jurisdictional Conference, to which both of us were elected delegates.

His book, *Christian Moral Judgment* and his method of positive moral presumption have shaped my teaching in Christian theology and social ethics. What have continued to resonate with me from Wogaman's method of positive moral presumption are his assertions pertaining to: (1) the goodness of created existence; (2) the value of human life; (3) the unity of the human family; and (4) the equality of all persons in God.

In relinquishing his clergy credentials, Wogaman's reference to Dietrich Bonhoeffer's beckoning us to practice "costly discipleship" leads me to deeper introspection as to what it would mean and look like - what it would cost each of us - to be a part of moving the church farther along toward becoming fully inclusive of all persons.

At our annual conference, we were asked by one of the plenary speakers to share with others what we see as an image that characterizes the church today. My response was that I see the image of a fault line that lies just below the surface. The fault line is something that might not be seen, but it is there with the potential of coming to the fore and dividing and breaking apart that which is already cracked.

With the work of our denomination's Commission on the Way Forward underway, my hope and prayer is that our denomination and its structures will see in the Commission's proposal ways that we can invite, welcome, offer radical hospitality and affirm God's gifts in each of us who are created by the same God, serve the same God, and are called into the ministries of the lay and clergy by the same God.

My hopes and prayers are that we will somehow find ways to move toward becoming what the prophet Isaiah envisions as God's peaceable realm (Isa. 11:6), God's *Beloved Community*.

13 - WHAT'S NEXT? CHAOS OR COMMUNITY?
(An Essay)

(This article was published in the United Methodist Connection of the United Methodist Church, Fulton, MD in June 2018)

I am a fifth generation Methodist. I sense that one of the primary reasons that my family members before me remained in Methodist churches - worshipped and served faithfully, and steadfastly supported them - was because of hope. They had hope that despite racism, gender bias and social stratification - the stated leanings toward grace and inclusion that were theological precepts and practices of Methodism's founder John Wesley lent themselves to their Methodist churches being places where all people could someday find a spiritual home in Christ.

In fact, John Wesley opposed and worked to eradicate the most egregious, dehumanizing social, spiritual American sin of his day – slavery, and its concomitant racism, notwithstanding the social teachings on race of the church of his ordination, the Anglican Church. Wesley preached and practiced a form of social holiness that evidenced that the world (all people) was his parish.

My family remained Methodist holding on to a hope that despite structural segregation and discrimination against Black, Brown and Native American people, women of all races, divorced persons, and others - the church would eventually live into a vision of real diversity and inclusion, and realize that what inclusivity really looks like is spaces where 'all people' really does mean 'all people'.

The reasons that my family members before me remained Methodists are the very same reasons that I choose to continue to live out my faith as a United Methodist today. With the recent gathering of the 234th session of the Baltimore-Washington Annual Conference in Baltimore, we experienced again that we are challenged to live into fully practicing what we say we believe that 'all people' means 'all people' when it comes to the full inclusion of our sisters and brothers who are LGBTQI+ as it regards membership, marriage equality, ordination and ministerial appointments. Again, the Annual Conference refused to commission and ordain LGBTQI+ persons who have presented themselves to the Church for service in these capacities, and were approved and recommended by the Baltimore-Washington Conference Board of Ordained Ministry.

In reflecting on the current state of United Methodism, the questions that reside with me are first if it will ever be possible for the United Methodist Church to move beyond its current place of division around the matter of full inclusion of all persons - including those who are LGBTQI+ - in the life of the church, and if so, at what costs.

For me, as chairperson of the Baltimore-Washington Conference Board of Ordained Ministry, a member of the Order of Elders, a local pastor, and most importantly as a disciple and servant of Jesus Christ, my conscience compels me to write, speak and act regarding this. It was Dietrich Bonhoeffer who intimated to the German churches in the 1940's, amidst the injustices and atrocities of Nazi Germany directed at Jewish, LGBTQI+, "non-white" people and others that "not to speak is to speak, and not to act is to act."

In his 1963 Letter from Birmingham Jail, Martin Luther King, Jr. distinguished between a just and an unjust law: "Any law that uplifts human personality is just. Any law that degrades human personality is unjust." In King's words: "A just law is a man-made code that squares with the moral law or the law of God. An unjust law is a code that is out of harmony with the 'moral law'." According to him, unjust laws downgrade the individual, and make distinctions between different 'groups' of people.

He based his understanding of just and unjust laws largely on the teachings of Thomas Aquinas on natural law in *Summa Theologica*. King further intimated that "One has not only a legal but a moral responsibility to obey just laws. Conversely one has a moral responsibility to disobey unjust laws". This is the nature of civil (and holy) disobedience.

I believe that this is what the proposed UMC "Traditional Plan" does, and thus I believe that the "Traditional Plan" is ad hominem with moral law and is unjust. Many persons who, at this juncture, advocate for the full inclusion of LGBTQI+ persons in the Church believe that the 46 years (since 1972) of exclusionary policies contained in the United Methodist Church's Book of Discipline, and the resultant exclusionary practices are effectively (church) laws that are unjust.

King's Birmingham Jail letter was written to address eight white clergymen (two of whom were Methodist) and their churches and synagogues that in 1963 were insisting on gradual, moderate approaches to change in addressing the atrocious racial and social injustices occurring in Birmingham, Alabama and across the nation at that time. Then, a few months after the Birmingham letter, at the March on Washington, DC in August 1963, King again addressed the matters of gradualism and moderation, and argued for immediacy, and the "fierce urgency of now" in acting against unjust laws, and seeking to move toward racial, social and economic justice for all people. He said, "We are now faced with the fact that tomorrow is today. We are confronted with the fierce urgency of now."

I sense that along with a clear sense of their faithfulness, fruitfulness, fitness and readiness for the ministries of Deacon and Elder in the United Methodist Church, this same sense of immediacy and the fierce urgency of now around affirming God's calling on LGBTQI+ persons to serve in ordained ministry is the spirit in which the Baltimore-Washington Conference Board of Ordained Ministry earlier this year conducted our full inquiry of candidates presented to us, and arrived at our prayerful decisions to recommend 29 persons for commissioning and ordination, including 2 persons who identify as LGBTQI+.

Two questions that persist for me are (1) what Jesus might do, and (2) what is Jesus doing as it regards the full inclusion of LGBTQI+ persons in the life of the United Methodist Church? In some of his first recorded public words, Jesus said, *"The Spirit of the Lord is upon me. God has anointed me to bring good news to the poor. God has sent me to proclaim freedom for the prisoners and recovery of sight for the blind, to set the oppressed free, to proclaim the year of the Lord's favor"* (Luke 4:18-19). Then, over the next three years, Jesus went about acting on what he said he believed.

65

I believe that Jesus would act today in ways that unconditional love and grace are demonstrated and extended to all persons, and that he'd act in ways that all persons who are on the margins of the Church and society are welcome and fully included in the Church's life. And I believe that if Jesus deemed laws and rules to be unjust and harmful today, he would necessarily resist, reject and disobey them (as he did in his day) for the sake of the kin-dom of God. This is the nature of civil (and holy) disobedience.

As it pertains to the full inclusion of LGBTQI+ and all persons in the life of the United Methodist Church, the path forward now leads to St. Louis, Missouri, the called session General Conference in February 2019, and consideration of the recommendation of the Council of Bishops and its Commission on the Way Forward. My fervent prayer is that in the weeks and months to come, God's Spirit will move in ways that make it clear what the Church's commitments are, in our words and actions, as to the full inclusion of all persons in all facets of the Church's life.

14 - HOPE FOR TOMORROW *(A Sermon)*

Also, seek the peace and prosperity of the city to which I have carried you into exile. Pray to the LORD for it, because if it prospers, you too will prosper." Yes, this is what the LORD Almighty, the God of Israel, says: "Do not let the prophets and diviners among you deceive you. Do not listen to the dreams you encourage them to have. They are prophesying lies to you in my name. I have not sent them," declares the LORD. This is what the LORD says: "When seventy years are completed for Babylon, I will come to you and fulfill my good promise to bring you back to this place. For I know the plans I have for you," declares the LORD, "plans to prosper you and not to harm you, plans to give you hope and a future. (Jer. 29:7-11)

I've come to discover that some things in life bear repeating. Some things are so important (integral) to who we are that they bear reiterating so that they sink deep into our spirit.

One of those fundamental truths of life as to who we are and who God is for us is that God is a God of hope. Hope is a part of the very character and nature of who God is.

And as people of faith, people in relationship with God, we are not only called to be in connection with who God is, but we - you and I - are called to be the bearers of hope in the world.

We are to be the progenitors of hope here on earth, carrying hope – sharing hope with a world that often seems to find itself near hopelessness. Dr. Martin Luther King, Jr.

intimated in one of his later sermons, "The Meaning of Hope, that *"hope is that quality which is necessary for life."*

Indeed, we need hope to be fully alive. There is much around us that might lead some of us to believe that we are living on the edge – living near hopelessness. With so much that lies in wait to discourage us and lead us toward despair, with so much that stands to leave us at points of disillusionment and disappointment – with the many trials and tribulations that we all face – with struggles and stumbling blocks that confront us – with the valleys and vicissitudes that come our way – *it's easy to feel at times that we are teetering on the edge of despair - near hopelessness.*

But with God, whose very character and nature is filled with hope, we are never really at the point of hopelessness. Old Testament scholar Walter Brueggemann in his book *The Prophetic Imagination* says that *"... hope is subversive, for it limits the grandiose pretension of the present, daring to announce that the present to which we have all made commitments is now called into question."*

Jeremiah's ministry was carried out among a people 2600 years ago who found themselves at a place on the edge - near hopelessness. For 70 years, Israel found itself in Babylonian exile – separated from their home and hopes – separated from any sense of promise and possibility for their future.

That's why Jeremiah was known as the lamenting prophet. That's why he was known to cry and lament over the condition of the people. That's what despair will do, won't it? It will make us want to cry, if not holler.

We recall that Jesus wept when he thought about the condition of Jerusalem.

Jeremiah lamented and cried about the condition of his people. I can remember serving as a United Methodist district superintendent in Baltimore in 2007, and being called into the Bishop's office. His question for me was, simply, *what are we (you) going to do about Baltimore?* That year, there were 278 murders in Baltimore. Those were 278 people whose loved ones – parents, spouses, children and siblings were left to grieve.

The corollaries to this spiking murder rate were ongoing poverty rates in east, west and south Baltimore, difficulties and underachievement in most public schools, high rates of un- and under-employment, and high rates of drug addiction. *And the Bishop's question to me was a simple, but really not so simple one – "what are we (you) going to do about Baltimore?"*

What emerged was a plan, imbedded with a promise. With God's leading, we named the plan "Hope for the City", an initiative designed to strengthen churches and communities in Baltimore. The interesting thing about "Hope for the City" is that many people thought we were crazy to be saying that God had given us hope for the city of Baltimore in the midst of the near hopelessness in which we found ourselves in 2007.

But what we are assured of is that God never leaves us with a predicament where there is no promise and no hope. Jeremiah realized this. God gave him a word to encourage the people.

Jeremiah told them, (in the near hopeless situation you find yourselves), *"seek the peace and prosperity of the city where you find yourselves"*... and then Jeremiah concluded with a word from the Lord, *"For I know the plans I have for you,"* declares the LORD, *"plans to prosper you and not to harm you, plans to give you a future with hope." (Jeremiah 29: 7,11)*

The Good News is that this hope for tomorrow, this future with hope that Jeremiah told the people about is the same hope that has animated people of faith over centuries.

Jeremiah's hope for the future of Israel is the same hope that Martin Luther King, Jr. talked about in "The Meaning of Hope". He asserted that hope was the *"refusal to give up despite overwhelming odds."* He said that hope is to be viewed as "*animated and undergirded by faith and love.*" In King's mind, if you had hope, you had faith in something.

As we walk by faith, we walk in hope. As we walk in God's grace, we walk in hope. We walk believing that hope will carry us into our future. We walk believing that our tomorrows will be better than our today. We walk believing that our best days and most blessed days are not behind us, but ahead of us.

We are the bearers, the carriers of hope. Our lives and our future depend on hope. Might we live this hope in that days ahead.

SECTION TWO

15 - A PRAYER FOR THE NATION AND WORLD

(We, the people of Epworth Chapel, Baltimore join others in prayers of thanksgiving and prayers for the nation on the eve of Thanksgiving, 2016.)

"God of our weary years, God of our silent tears; thou who has brought us thus far along the way. Thou who has by thy might, led us into the light - keep us forever in thy path we pray." (James Weldon Johnson)

O God, you see all and know all – and amidst the various and sundry vicissitudes of life, we are mindful that you are in control of all that is and is to be. Today, we offer thanks to you for your steadfast love toward us. We are a people of divergent perspectives, with diversities of hopes, dreams and visions. But we come before you acknowledging the commonality that we all share in you, the creator of the entire universe.

O God, we offer you thanks for this nation, and we take this opportunity to offer prayers for the nation and our world. We pray for the people of every city and county in every state in America. We pray that you would bless every home and every community - every school and every place where your people gather for work and leisure. Bless those persons who are older and those who are younger. We pray for peace and safety for all of us who live and move throughout every community across our nation, and we pray likewise for communities like ours around the world.

Lord God, we pray especially for your blessings upon those persons who bear the burdens of want and disparity among us - whether it be for lack of food, shelter or clean water, inadequate healthcare or inadequate education.

We ask your blessings upon those who serve and lead the nation in elective and appointive office, and those who will do so in the future. Bless them with a portion of your wisdom, patience, integrity, humility, justice and compassion.

"Now dot thy still dews of quietness; let all of our strivings cease; take now from our souls the strain and the stress; and let our ordered lives confess; the beauty of your peace." (John Greenleaf Whittier)

16 - WHAT BECOMES OF THE BROKEN-HEARTED? *(A Sermon)*

My God, my God, why have you forsaken me? Why are you so far from saving me, so far from my cries of anguish? My God, I cry out by day, but you do not answer, by night, but I find no rest. Yet you are enthroned as the Holy One; you are the one Israel praises. In you our ancestors put their trust; they trusted and you delivered them. To you they cried out and were saved; in you they trusted and were not put to shame. (Psalm 22:1-5)

If I can be transparent for a few moments, there have been only a few times in my life when I have been truly broken-hearted. One was when our son, Marcus William Hunt died from an accidental drowning on August 7, 2005. Another was on September 11, 2001, with the terrorist attacks on the World Trade Center in New York City, in Pennsylvania and at the Pentagon in Virginia. Yet another was with the assassination of Rev. Dr. Martin Luther King, Jr. on April 4, 1968. And a fourth time was at the United States presidential election on November 8-9, 2016.

If you've ever been broken-hearted, you know what it feels like, and you can feel the same pain that I'm still experiencing in the aftermath of the election. To be clear this is not, at its core, a political concern – it is more an existential concern – getting to the very core of who I am, and who *we* are as people of God.

Indeed, many of us right now are living with broken spirits - broken hopes and dreams - broken hearts. It would not be an overstatement to declare that the experience of broken-heartedness is often accompanied by a sense that one has been *punched in the gut* so hard, and knocked down to the point that one finds it difficult to get back up. The broken-heartedness that I'm talking about carries with it profound disappointment, dis-heartedness, confusion and pain – and indeed fear for the future of God's creation. This brokenness often leads to bitter tears of despair, which may seem to drip with no end in sight.

At its core, this broken-heartedness is connected with a wonder about where God is in all of what has occurred. Is God present? Does God care? If so, how and why would God allow that which threatens good for God's people to occur?

This is what the psalmist in Psalm 22 sought to address. As we make our way to this song, we find ourselves parked at *a blues song.* The psalmist – who most scholars believe was David – *was singing the blues* – and he asked God a question, *"Why Lord, have you forsaken me?* These are the very same words that Jesus uttered on Calvary's cross as recorded in Matthew 27 and Mark 15, *"My God, my God. Why have you forsaken me?"*

David, indeed, was singing a sorrow song. If we were to talk to David today, he might tell us that something terrible had gone on in his life that served to break his heart. Maybe it was the death of a loved one. It could have been a relationship that he thought would never end, that did. It could have been something, anything, that he never expected to happen, that did happen. He asked, *"Why Lord?"*

Whatever "it" was for David, it served to break his heart, and led him into a deep theological, spiritual and existential conundrum. "Why, God would you allow this -

74

whatever *this* is - to happen to me, a person of faith? You are the very same God in whom my parents put their trust, and you blessed them saved them - but now I am going through this." *"Why Lord?"*

Indeed, the theological and spiritual conundrum that we find ourselves in as a nation and as the church today is a concern of theodicy – which points to the question of the very justice and fairness of God. A fundamental theological and spiritual question for people of faith today is, *"Why Lord?"*

"God, why?" "Why, if you are a good and loving God, would you allow bad things to happen to your people (any of your people)?" *"Why God,* do you allow evil - racism, sexism, classism, xenophobia, militarism, misogyny, homophobia, anti-Semitism, Islamophobia - to exist and persist among us?"

God, why? Even for good people – faithful people - this question, *"Why?"* is real. At the prolonged illness of his own son, Rabbi Harold Kushner wrote a book in 1981, *"When Bad Things Happen to Good People",* in which he sought to address this very profound faith and existential question, *"Why Lord?"*

It is a perennial question. *God, why?* Somehow, for some reason - on the existential, theological and moral spectrum, God allows evil to exist in our world. God *is* all-powerful and all-present, and yet evil exists. God is all-caring and all-knowing, and yet we get sick… loved ones die... persons remain hungry… homeless… hurting… and in need of help.

In 1966, the late soul singer, Jimmy Ruffin posed this concern about the broken-hearted in a song -
> *(refrain)*
> *Now what becomes of the brokenhearted*
> *Who has love that's now departed?*
> *I know I've got to find*
> *Some kind of peace of mind…*

What becomes of the broken-hearted? To answer this question, the only thing that we who walk by faith can put our trust, confidence and hope in is the fact that just as God did not foreclose on David and the Israelites - God does not, will not foreclose on you and me.

In these days, we must put our faith, trust and hope even more in Almighty God – and believe even more than ever before that *the arc of the moral universe is long, but it (always) bends toward justice.* We must believe now more than ever before that if we do our part – if we pray without ceasing… if we love unconditionally…. if we work while it's day – God will do what God has always done, and save God's people.

The only way to square this matter of broken-heartedness, the only way that this can make sense, *is to believe that in the midst of mourning, God must be somewhere, somehow, working things out.* The only thing that can bring joy in sorrow is a belief beyond belief that God is working in the midst of mourning and sorrow to make things right.

What becomes of the broken-hearted? Some good news is that David lived to sing something other than the blues - *and so will we.* David sang at other places –

- *"If it had not been of the Lord, who was on our side, where would we be? (Psalm 124:1-2)*
- *"I've been young, and I've been old, but I've never seen the righteous forsaken – or God's seed begging for bread." (Psalm 37:25)*
- *"Weeping may endure for a night – but joy will come in the morning!" (Psalm 30:5)*

What becomes of the broken-hearted? For those of us who walk by faith and not by sight, we live with the blessed assurance that amidst life's adversities and adversaries, God shows up and protects us and positions us for new possibilities:

- Our present position may be brokenness, but God's possibility is healing.
- We might be facing stumbling blocks, but God has already positioned stepping stones for us.
- Amidst our haters, God has already positioned elevators in our lives.
- In the midst of need and want, God's possibility for our lives says that we will be the lender and not a borrower.
- Our possibility is to be the head and not the tail.

Thanks be to God who cares for us. Thanks be to God who mends broken hearts. Thanks be to God who does not foreclose on us, and indeed comes to see about the broken-hearted!

17 - ECCLESIAL JUSTICE: THE PROBLEM OF SUNDAY MORNING AND MOVING TOWARDS THE BELOVED COMMUNITY

(This is the manuscript of a plenary lecture delivered to the Doctor of Ministry program at United Theological Seminary, Dayton, Ohio, August 23, 2018.)

The world today is fraught with social, economic, political and religious upheaval. Over the past several years, in the United States and across the globe, we have become more divided along various lines. In the U.S., the social and political division that we now experience is not really new, but it challenges our sense of normalcy in ways that perhaps we have not been challenged in the past.

About seven years ago, I was asked, in another academic setting, to address the matter of "Sunday Morning", and to answer the question, "Is it the most segregated the hour of the week? This is what I deem to be "the Problem of Sunday Morning". I believe that this is a matter that continues to weigh on the churches in many respects today. And so, the questions today are: (1) what does ecclesial justice look like in the 21st century, (2) how might we go about addressing "the Problem of Sunday Morning", and (3) what would it look like for the churches, as the Body of Christ (the embodiment of Christ), to move towards becoming the *Beloved Community*?

I propose that a great deal of the problem of Sunday Morning, and division in and among churches today, is rooted in the persistent problem of racism in America. Thus, it is important that division in the churches, and particularly race division, be understood against the historical backdrop of the racism in American society, in general.

In 1903, African-American sociologist W. E. B. DuBois pronounced that "the problem of the 20th century is the problem of the color-line (*The Souls of Black Folk*). In 1944, Swedish sociologist Gunnar Myrdal chronicled the plight of African Americans (the Negro Problem) within the context of what he referred to as the "American dilemma" (*An American Dilemma: The Negro Problem and Modern Democracy)*. And in 1968, the Kerner Commission Report, based on a study which President Lyndon B. Johnson had requested in light of the civil unrest and riots that had broken out in several cities across the United States, summarized the state of race relations in America by noting that "America is a nation of two societies, one black and one white, separate and unequal." This reality continues to exist some 50 years later.

During a visit to the Southern Poverty Law Center in Montgomery, AL in early 2018, I and others who were a part of the visit were informed that there are over 954 hate-related groups currently identified in the U.S., up from about 800 in 2008, and this number has continued to rise since the 2016 presidential election. This rise in hate-related groups in America (and the incumbent violence) is viewed against the historic backdrop of the lynching of over 4000 Black Americans in 10 Southern states from 1870-1950, as chronicled by the Equal Justice Initiative, also in Montgomery, Alabama. According to the Southern Poverty Law Center, the number of

79

neo-Nazi groups in the U.S. has increased by 22 percent since the 2017 U.S. presidential inauguration.

Today, race continues to matter in America, and indeed we are not yet at the place of being either post-racial or post-racist. This is the matter that Michael Eric Dyson addresses in his book, *Can You Hear Me Now?* Dyson insists that the critical question that is before society today is not if we are yet a *post-racial* society, and the question is not even if we should strive to become post-racial, but the question is how might we move closer to becoming a *post-racist* society?

A part of America's sense of who it says it is is etched in one of our national credos – the Latin phrase *e-pluribus unum* – "Out of Many One." The implication here is that in the U.S, we have been, and continue to be, many. We are many cultures and ethnicities (we are a nation largely made up of immigrants and refugees), many classes and social locations, many religions, many geographies, female and male, with many persuasions and ways of identifying what it means to be human. And yet, the vision that we say we share within the context of this "many" is a vision of somehow also becoming "one".

In any event, today we experience the challenge of living into this grand vision of what it means to become *e pluribus unum*. And so, perhaps it is "divides" in the churches and society which most clearly characterize us today. These "divides" are seen in that we are Indigenous, Hispanic, Asian, White and Black, LGBTQI+ and "straight", poor, working class, middle class and wealthy, Republican, Democratic and Independent, southern and northern, western and eastern, midwestern and southwestern, rural, suburban and urban, conservative, moderate and liberal, evangelical and progressive, non-denominational and mainline. These "divides" are seen in that – politically and religiously - we are red, blue and indeed purple (yes purple).

In light of an image and ideal of social embodiment and social justice, and in light of the church's image of it being the body of Christ (the embodiment of Christ), the question then becomes how do various forms of difference, division, disintegration and disengagement effectively serve to create social and spiritual disembodiment for us in the churches and society? In her book, *Stand Your Ground: Black Bodies and the Justice of God,* Kelly Brown Douglas posits that such disembodiment can be seen through the crucifixion of Jesus on the Cross, and the death of Trayvon Martin in Florida in 2012. "Both Jesus and Trayvon were members of despised minorities. Both were feared because of who they were... Both were accused of sedition. Both were killed by the "rule of law."[8]

Such disembodiment is seen in even more pronounced ways in the rhetorical and existential attacks on women's bodies in some of the highest places of our society today – in politics, entertainment, sports and even the church. As Cheryl Townsend Gilkes intimates in her essay, "The Loves and Troubles of African American Women's Bodies" -

"All human experience is embodied experience and the consequences of cultural humiliation are most dramatically shown with reference to the body. Not only is experience embodied, but stereotypes, pernicious

---

[8] Kelly Brown Douglas, *Stand Your Ground: Black Bodies and the Justice of God* (Maryknoll, NY: Orbis Books, 2015), 170.

81

cultural representations of people, are also embodied images."[9]

Why is this important in the light of the practice of theology and ministry today?

Steven Vertovec, in his essay, "Super-diversity and Its Implications", places the phenomenon of social change in the context of what he terms 'super-diversity'. Although Vertovec focuses primarily on the changing dynamics of diversity in Britain, these changes, in many respects, mirror the changes occurring in the United States.[10]

Vertovec argues that today, "Britain can now be characterized by 'super-diversity,' a notion intended to underline a level and kind of complexity surpassing anything the country has previously experienced…"

"… where in the past Britain's immigrant and ethnic minority population has conventionally been characterized by large, well-organized African-Caribbean and South Asian communities of citizens originally from Commonwealth countries or formerly colonial territories."

Vertovec's thesis of "super-diversity" holds with what has occurred in the United States over the past several decades. Research data shows that the United States continues to become

---

[9] Cheryl Townsend Gilkes, "The Loves and Troubles of African American Women's Bodies" in *A Troubling in My Soul,* Emilie M. Townes, ed. (Maryknoll, NY: Orbis, 1993), 232.

[10] Steven Vertovec, "Super-diversity and Its Implications," *Ethnic and Racial Studies* 30, no. 6 (2007): 1024-1054.

more diverse and "different". Our difference in the U.S. is seen in that –

- The non-Hispanic white population in the U.S. is expected to fall below 50% by 2042, but non-Hispanic Whites will remain the largest single ethnic group (U.S. Census Bureau).
- Non-Hispanic Whites are the slowest growing segment of the U.S. population at .5% (U.S. Census Bureau).
- There are at least 56 million Hispanics in the U.S. (16% of the population). Hispanic populations are projected to make up 30% of the U.S. population by 2050 (U.S. Census Bureau).
- Asians make up 5.8% of the U.S. population, and this percentage is projected to rise to at least 7.8% by 2050. Asians make up 36% of immigrants, exceeding the percentage of Hispanics. China is the fastest growing immigrant group in the U.S., passing Mexico (U.S. Census Bureau).
- The percentage of Blacks is projected to remain steady at 13% through 2050.
- By 2040, Islam will surpass Judaism to become the second largest religion in the U.S. due to higher immigration and birth rates (Pew Research Center).
- There are at least 3.3 million Muslims in the U.S., and that number is likely to double by 2050 (Pew Research Center).

(Sources: U.S. Census Bureau and Pew Research Center)

This is what super-diversity in the U.S. will continue to look like.

Biblical and Theological Reflections

How might our biblical and theological analysis speak to these realities? A careful reading of scripture points with clarity to God's divine design for all of humanity. The assertion that God has created all of humanity in God's image was first recorded in scripture in the Book of Genesis, and reminds us that God's purpose for us is rooted in our God-likeness and the notion that we as humans are created *imago dei,* in God's image.   And it is in our God-likeness that we find our commonality in Christ.

Instances of the yearning towards ecclesial justice – communal justice - can be found throughout Scripture.   We find it in the Prophet Isaiah's vision of the peaceable realm, where *wolves and lambs would lie down together* (Isa. 11:6). We see this yearning for ecclesial and communal justice in the Prophet Micah's explication of what has come to be known as the Great Requirement, that we are to *"love kindness, do justice and walk humbly with God"* (Micah 6:8).

God's will and desire for ecclesial, communal justice – for the church and world - is further evidenced in the words of the psalmist as found in Psalm 133.

> *How very good and pleasant it is when kindred live together in unity! It is like the precious oil on the head, running down upon the beard, on the beard of Aaron, running down over the collar of his robes. It is as if the dew of Hermon were falling down on Mount Zion. For*

*there the Lord ordained God's blessing, life forevermore
(Psalm 133:1-3).*

The psalm speaks to the whole family of God, and reminds us of God's ideal that we break down barriers and walls of division, and join with those who have been estranged from fellowship with God and God's people. One important thing to notice is that the psalmist points to the blessing of not simply dwelling together, but *dwelling together in unity*. Certainly, the psalmist could have stopped by saying that it is good that we dwell together, but he went on to share that it's very good and pleasant in God's sight when we *dwell together in unity*. *"For there the Lord ordained God's blessing, life forevermore" (Ps. 133:3).*

In *The Search for Common Ground*, Howard Thurman asserted that the search for common ground is a universal search among all of humanity. He stated that "A person is always threatened in one's very ground by a sense of isolation, by feeling oneself cut off from one's fellows. Yet, the person can never separate oneself from one's fellows, for mutual interdependence is characteristic of all life."[11] Thus, for Thurman, this common, universal quest and search for common ground has teleological implications, as it essentially provides the framework for the meaning of life itself.

Desmond Tutu, in his nonviolent battle against apartheid in South Africa, rallied around the concept of *Ubuntu*, *"I am*

---

[11] Howard Thurman, *The Search for Common Ground: An Inquiry into the Basis of Man's Experience of Community* (Richmond, Indiana: Friends United Press, 1971), pp. 2-3.

what I am because of who we all are, and therefore, because of who we are, I am." Ubuntu speaks to the very quality of being human, affirms the fundamental humanness of all people, and asserts the support that we must afford each other if we are to be all that God calls us to be.

Ubuntu also speaks to the yearning toward community. Community – common ground – by its very nature - is integrative; it speaks to a "common unity" among us. Forms of disintegration, disunity and disembodiment are, therefore, to be understood as being antithetical and ad hominem with the common good, community and to the will of God.

In her book *Ferguson and Faith: Sparking Leadership and Awakening Community*, Leah Gunning Francis intimates that "The fight for justice… is the fight to be seen and valued as human beings "just as you are"- not in a prescribed way that renders you acceptable so long as you fit a particular mold, but in an authentic way that makes room for each person to be able to be fully him – or herself."[12]

The Churches and the Problem of Sunday Morning

In his 1954 book, *The Creative Encounter*, Howard Thurman reflected on the state of the church in his day, and stated:

It is in order now at last to raise the question: Is the witness of the church in our society the unfolding of such an idea as we see manifested in the religious experience

---

[12] Leah Gunning Francis, *Ferguson and Faith: Sparking Leadership and Awakening Community* (St. Louis, MO: Chalice Press, 2015), 109.

and the life of Jesus? Whatever may be the delimiting character of the historical development of the church, the simple fact remains that at the present moment in our society, as an institution, the church is divisive and discriminating, even within its fellowship. It is divided into dozens of splinters. This would indicate that it is essentially sectarian in character. As an institution there is no such thing as the church.[13]

As it regards Christianity and the church of his day, Thurman had written five years earlier in his seminal work *Jesus and the Disinherited* that:

To those who need profound succor and strength to enable them to live in the present with dignity and creativity, Christianity often has been sterile and of little avail. The conventional Christian word is muffled, confused and vague. Too often the price exacted by society for security and respectability is that the Christian movement in its formal expression must be on the side of the strong against the weak. This is a matter of tremendous significance, for it reveals to what extent a religion that was born of people acquainted with persecution and suffering has become the cornerstone of a civilization and of nations whose very position in

---

[13] Howard Thurman, *The Creative Encounter: An Interpretation of Religion and The Social Witness* (Richmond, IN: Friends United Press, 1954), 139.

modern life has too often been secured by ruthless use of power applied to weak and defenseless people.[14]

Thurman saw that the problem of an excluding church is rooted in the fact that too many Christians have not clearly understood or faithfully followed the central personality of the faith, Jesus Christ. Further, Thurman insisted that racism is one of the key factors incumbering community. For him, community is essential to life, and it is this that moved and motivated Thurman. It is out of this deep sense of burden and passion for community that Thurman was able to see how detrimental and destructive racism and other forms of social division are to community because they deny, denigrate and destroy people based on external and surface qualities. *This is the essence of social and spiritual disembodiment.*

As it regards the church and the problem of racism and other forms of social disembodiment in America today, in many ways, a pall remains over much – if not most - of the contemporary church and society. *Racism continues to be the elephant in America's living room.* In their book, *Divided by Faith: Evangelical Religion and the Problem of Race,* Michael Emerson and Christian Smith developed a theory to explain why churches are racially exclusive enclaves despite Christianity's ideals and espoused beliefs about being inclusive.

According to Emerson and Smith, Americans choose where and with whom to worship; race is one of the most important grounds on which they choose; so, the more choices

---

[14] See Howard Thurman, *Jesus and the Disinherited,* (Richmond, IN: Friends United Press, 1969), 89-109.

they have, the more their religious institutions will be segregated.[15]

Through sociological analysis, Emerson and Smith tested their thesis and found it to be valid. Churches are more segregated than schools, workplaces or neighborhoods. The least segregated sector of American society is also the least governed by choice; it's the military. Because white Protestants are the largest religious community in the U.S., they have the greatest choice as to with whom to gather. The authors point out that ninety-five percent of churches are effectively racially segregated, with 80 percent or more of their members being of the same race.

Thus, about 5 percent of religious congregations in the U.S. can fairly be considered multicultural/multiracial, with the majority of Christians engaging in what sociologists call homophily, or the desire to congregate with "birds of the same feather," with their congregations reflecting ethnoracial particularism.

Lovett Weems from Wesley Theological Seminary points to the correlation between church decline and the problems that churches face in addressing race and class. *"In the last two decades, five mainline denominations had a net loss of over 5.2 million members, while the population of the country rose by over 47 million. The figures are even worse when one looks at people of color and people in poverty."*

---

[15] Michael Emerson and Smith, Christian, *Divided by Faith: Evangelical Religion and the Problem of Race,* Oxford, UK: Oxford University Press, 2000), 154f.

Towards the Beloved Community

How might we go about moving towards the realization of the *Beloved Community*? It is important to note that the singular theological and societal vision of Howard Thurman and Martin Luther King, Jr. was for the realization of the *Beloved Community*. For King, the *Beloved Community* is rooted in the biblical notion of *Agape* (God's unconditional love), and is to be the ultimate goal for society and the church.

In one of his chapters in *On God's Side*, Jim Wallis posits that "The Beloved Community Welcomes All Tribes."[16] Wallis shares a quote from King that "our goal is to create a beloved community and this will require a qualitative change in our souls as well as a quantitative change in our lives."

King asserted that "all life is interrelated." One of his fundamental beliefs was in the kinship of all persons. He believed that all life is part of a single process; all living things are interrelated; and all persons are sisters and brothers.[17] All have a place in the *Beloved Community*. Because all life is interrelated, one cannot harm another without harming oneself. King elaborated:

> To the degree that I harm my brother, no matter what he is doing to me, to that extent I am harming myself. For example, white men often refuse federal aid to education in order to avoid giving the Negro his rights; but because all men are brothers, they cannot deny Negro

[16] Jim Wallis, *On God's Side: What Religion Forgets and Politics Hasn't Learned about Serving the Common Good* (Grand Rapids, MI: Brazos Press, 2013), 109.

[17] Garth Baker-Fletcher, *Somebodyness: Martin Luther King, Jr. and the Theory of Dignity* (Minneapolis, MN: Fortress Press, 1993), 132.

children without harming themselves. Why is this? Because all men are brothers. If you harm me, you harm yourself. Love, *agape*, is the only cement that can hold this broken community together. When I am commanded to love, I am commanded to restore community, to resist injustice, and to meet the needs of my brothers.[18]

Over the past 20 years, I have had the opportunity to lead and teach seminary students from several theological institutions in the study of the Civil Rights movement, nonviolence, community-building and the *Beloved Community* in Alabama, and across other parts of the southern United States.

Our groups usually range from 15-30 graduate students, and in Alabama, we travel through Birmingham, Montgomery and Selma retracing the steps of those who participated in the American Civil Rights movement in the 1950s and 60s. Our groups are invariably very diverse. We are typically women and men; Whites, Caribbeans, Native Americans, Hispanics, Asians, Africans and African Americans. We are typically from several different Christian denominations: United Methodist, Baptist, African Methodist Episcopal, African Methodist Episcopal Zion, Episcopalian, Lutheran and others, along with persons from Muslim, Jewish and Hindu faith communities.

We begin each day with singing, praying and reading Scripture, as was the practice in the tradition among those who participated in the Civil Rights movement. John Lewis, now a U.S. Congressman from Georgia, and one who labored on the

---

[18] Baker-Fletcher, 132.

front lines of the movement in the 1960's, has intimated that "We never went out without singing and praying." So before leaving each morning, those of us on these immersion trips pray, read Scripture, and sing freedom songs like "Oh Freedom," "We Shall Overcome," "There is a Balm" and "Ain't Gonna Let Nobody Turn Me Around".

As we travel, struggling through many of the difficult paths and realities of those who lived the Civil Rights movement and labored through it, we invariably sense among ourselves the real possibility that culturally inclusive community – the *Beloved Community* – can indeed be realized in our lifetime.

We visit and study at numerous sites that were significant to the Civil Rights movement. In Montgomery, we visit Dexter Avenue King Memorial Baptist Church, where Rev. Dr. Martin Luther King, Jr. served as pastor from 1954-1960 at the height of the Montgomery Bus Boycott and other significant Civil Rights events. Just two blocks from Dexter Avenue Church, we visit the First Confederate White House - the home of Jefferson Davis, the president of the Confederacy. Sitting between Dexter Avenue Church and the first Confederate White House is the Alabama State Capitol – the place where in the 1960s Governor George Wallace and other state officials stood in defiance of any efforts towards integration and equal rights among the races, and where Wallace notoriously exclaimed, *"Segregation now, segregation tomorrow, segregation forever."*

In Birmingham, one of the places we visit is the Sixteenth Street Baptist Church, which on September 15, 1963 was bombed by segregationists, and where four black girls (ages 11-14) were killed in the church basement while preparing for their Children's Day worship celebration. Across the street from the Sixteenth Street Baptist Church is Kelly Ingram Park, where several of the protest marches in the city of Birmingham began, and which became notorious for the atrocious and brutal acts of Police Commissioner Eugene "Bull" Connor and the Birmingham police as they turned dogs and fire hoses on black children of Birmingham.

In Selma, we walk across the Edmund Pettus Bridge, which was the site of "Bloody Sunday" on March 7, 1965 - when hundreds of blacks and some whites gathered in an effort to march across the bridge towards Montgomery to demand voting rights, only to be violently tear-gassed, cattle-prodded, bloodily beaten and turned back by state and local authorities. In Selma, we also visit Brown Chapel African Methodist Episcopal Church, the place where over 600 persons gathered to sing, pray, strategize and receive marching orders in their ongoing efforts to take the 54-mile journey from Selma to Montgomery.

At the conclusion of these immersion experiences in Alabama – what I have deemed to be pilgrimages – we are invariably struck by how far we as a society have come, and yet how far we have to go. We realize that it would not have been possible 50 years prior for 15-30 ministers from diverse backgrounds to travel in relative peace and safety throughout Alabama. Furthermore, we realize that all of us – women, men, black, white, Asian, Native American and Latinx - either had, or were likely to obtain doctoral and master's degrees from major theological schools, and that this would not have been a realistic prospect 50 years ago.

Each time we journey, my memory harkens back to one of our trips several years ago, where Dr. Eileen Guenther, a professor at Wesley Theological Seminary, who was a part of that study group, offered that it was a spiritual sung by many choirs, "I'm Gonna Sit at the Welcome Table," that played in her head throughout our experience.[19] These tables are –

- *Lunch counters of restaurants where all had not been welcome (in the past);*

- *The dining room table in the parsonage of Dexter Avenue Baptist Church, in Montgomery, where we were told, the Southern Christian Leadership Conference was formed;*

- *The kitchen table of the same parsonage where Dr. King searched his soul and felt God telling him to press on with his work (see King's sermon, "A Knock at Midnight");*

- *The tables at which the people at Sixteenth Street Baptist Church served us lunch, tables placed adjacent to the site of the tragic bombing in September 1963 that killed four young girls;*

- *The tables around which members of our group gathered to share stories as victims of discrimination, of their courageous work in the Civil Rights movement (and other freedom and human rights movements), and their lament over a lack of*

---

[19] See *The American Organist*, November 2008. "From the President", vol. 42, no. 11.

awareness of what was going on at that time in America's history.

- *Tables around which we laughed and cried together – celebrating how far we've come, yet realizing the pain inflicted upon those who made it possible for us to be able to sit at table together in light of those things that could yet still be in place to divide us.*

We also recognize that there is hope for the church and society in the fact that largely because of the heroic efforts of persons in places like Montgomery, Birmingham and Selma, Alabama, Jackson, Mississippi and Memphis, Tennessee - the Civil Rights Act was passed by Congress in 1964, and the Voting Rights Act was enacted in 1965, signed into law by a U.S. president who was a son of the American South, Lyndon Baines Johnson.

A Look to the Future

A few years ago, I attended a panel conversation of seminary students. This experience shed light on matters that might be given attention in thinking on the future of the churches, especially in the United States.

The first observation about this seminary panel was the diversity of the group. Five of the six panelists were in their 20's or early 30's. They had arrived at seminary from six different places – Chicago, New York City, the Dominican Republic, Zimbabwe, Mississippi and Virginia – and none had lived in the city where they were now attending seminary. They were United Methodist (4), AME (1), and Baptist (1).

95

They were Korean, Latinx, African, White and African-American. Four were women.

This diversity reflects that of this particular seminary at-large, and points to the fact that the church and society today looks quite different than it did 40-50 years ago, and that perhaps this type of broadening diversity is reflective of where the church of today and tomorrow may be moving, and thus what will be required of its future leaders.

As these six students reflected on their seminary experiences and how they thought their theological education would impact their future role as religious leaders, it was clear that each of them articulated a vision of the church and their role as a religious leader that would move the church beyond traditional notions of what it has been, and is to become, institutionally. And thus, theirs were visions that shifted conceptions of Christian ministry, and the ways in which church/religious leadership might be practiced in the future.

The collective insights/observations of these seminarians point to prospects of the 21st century church living into new and exciting forms of diversity, and prospects of churches of the future being shaped in ways that give impetus to several foundational concerns. Succinctly stated, these concerns are that:

1. The church must be led towards deeper, more intentional exploration and growth in the practice of *spiritual disciplines* as means towards deepening faith and creating community.
2. The church must engage in processes that encourage the ongoing development of competencies in the *art of*

leadership that are sensitive to cultural inclusion and the changes that are incumbent in new millennial reality.

3. The church must facilitate reflection/action relative to the burgeoning *globality* in our midst.

4. The church must facilitate an ongoing understanding and deeper engagement with *youth and young adult cultures (Millennials and Generation Z)*, which typically understand and appropriate the merging of cultures on levels that are more profound and pronounced than previous generations.

5. The church must facilitate constructive engagement and theological discourse across *cultures and theological/faith perspectives.*

6. The church must have the capacity to continue in organizing, developing and cultivating *strong partnerships and collaborations* (with students, local churches, judicatories, interfaith and non-religious entities).

7. The church must see technology as a gift of discipleship and evangelism to be faithfully and effectively used to reach people of all generations for the sake of the Gospel.

Conclusion

There's hope. As a society, we have made some progress in that we don't hear or read of as many overt and violent acts of racism as we did in the 1950s and 60s. The rights of African Americans, Asians, Hispanics, Native Americans, and other ethnic minorities, along with the rights of women and other historically marginalized persons have been enhanced in many ways, yet today, we know that there are miles that we yet have to travel.

Although segregation indeed continues to abound in many churches (as it does in many other sectors of society), I believe there is hope. Charles Marsh wrote in *The Beloved Community: How Faith Shapes Social Justice, from the Civil Rights Movement to Today,* "Eleven o'clock Sunday may be the most segregated hour of the week as far as any particular parish goes, but it is the most integrated hour of the week as far as the kingdom goes."[20] Once again Marsh writes:

> The hope that we must nurture is the hope that all will be made whole in the history of redemption and that together we will join hands and learn to live in the sobering light of God's promise.[21]

Indeed, there's hope. St. Augustine of Hippo intimated that *"Hope has two beautiful daughters – Anger and Courage. Anger at the way things are, and the Courage to change some of them."* Martin Luther King, Jr. said that *"hope is the refusal to give up despite insurmountable odds."* Further, King said that *"hope (as a theological form) is animated by faith and love."*

King also intimated that everybody can be great because everybody can serve. Indeed, as the late Congresswoman Shirley Chisolm and Mohammad Ali, among others intimated, our service is the rent that we pay for the space that we occupy on earth. We all have a role to play in helping the church and world become more just and inclusive.

---

[20] Charles Marsh, *The Beloved Community: How Faith Shapes Social Justice, from the Civil Rights Movement to Today* (New York: Basic Books, 2005), 215.
[21] Marsh, 212.

There is hope because it is God's will that we be the Body of Christ – the embodiment of the Resurrected One.

18 - A PRAYER FOR THE STATE OF MARYLAND

(This prayer was offered for the Maryland State Senate and State of Maryland, Annapolis, MD on Thursday, January 17, 2019)

Gracious, all-loving and all-wise God, with the busyness of this new day, we pause to offer thanks to you. We come from various places; and from these places, we come with divergent perspectives; and with these perspectives we come with a diversity of hopes and dreams and visions. But we come acknowledging that we gather in the commonality that all persons share in you, the creator of the universe.

O God, we offer you thanks for the great state of Maryland. We pray that in the days ahead, you would continue to bless every home and every community of this great state. Bless every school and every place where your people gather for work or leisure. Bless those persons who are older and those who are younger. Bless us from Cumberland to Salisbury, from Elkton to Leonardtown, and all around and between. Bless Baltimore and bless Annapolis. We pray for peace and safety for all of us who live and move throughout this state, and we pray likewise for communities like ours across our nation and world.

We pray that you will bless each of us gathered here. Most importantly, we ask your blessings upon those who serve and lead the state of Maryland in elective and appointive office. Bless them with a portion of wisdom, patience, integrity, courage, justice and compassion. Bless each of those who serve and lead that they will be forever mindful of a collective commitment to act in ways that facilitate the betterment of each person, each home, each school, each community, and each place of business and leisure in Maryland. God, be with each of us now and forever, we pray. Amen.

19 - *A HOPE THAT'S ALIVE (A Sermon)*

Peter, an apostle of Jesus Christ, To God's elect, exiles scattered throughout the provinces of Pontus, Galatia, Cappadocia, Asia and Bithynia, who have been chosen according to the foreknowledge of God the Father, through the sanctifying work of the Spirit, to be obedient to Jesus Christ and sprinkled with his blood: Grace and peace be yours in abundance. Praise be to the God and Father of our LORD Jesus Christ! In his great mercy he has given us new birth into a living hope through the resurrection of Jesus Christ from the dead. (1 Peter 1:1-3)

If the truth is told among us, none of us really likes to be around dead things. For if something is dead, or needs to die, it's really of little effect – of little use. The nature of life is that we yearn for those things which are alive. We want to be around life, and not death. Indeed, God's desire for us is life, and not death. Just as God breathed life into all of creation in the beginning, God wills that we be alive – full of life today.

I've learned that there's a difference between living, and living life to its fullest. Many people are living – walking and breathing, but are not fully alive. *Many people are just getting by day-to-day; they are physically alive, but their minds and spirits are not fully alive.*

Jesus said that *"I have come to give you life, and life more abundantly (John 10:10)."* The abundant life that Jesus was talking about was the God-kind of life. The word for life that Jesus used is *Zoe'*, which means the God-kind of life – the fullness of life, abundant life.

102

This abundant life that Jesus talked about is like unto what Howard Thurman was talking about when he insisted – *"Don't ask what the world needs. Ask what makes you come alive, and go do it. Because what the world needs is more people who have come alive."*

Indeed, there is something deep within each and every one of us that waits to come alive. We're living in a time when there is so much that lurks waiting to discourage us, disappoint us, disillusion us, disgust us, and disrupt our sense of who we really are. These things can serve to sap us of our joy, sap our love for one another, and sap our hope. Certainly, many people today might feel like they are near hopelessness with the various vicissitudes and valleys of life that they must confront.

Peter (1 Pet. 1:3) sought to address similar near hopelessness facing the people of his day. They wondered what was to come of their faith, with Christ, the one in whom they had placed their faith and trust, no longer with them. Peter wrote to remind the Christians of his day that they had a living hope through the resurrection of Jesus Christ from the dead. *They had hope that's alive.*

Likewise, we are reminded that we have a hope that's alive. Our hope is not a dead hope, but is a hope that is alive. How could this be? It is because the same Christ who Peter talked about is the same Christ whom we worship today. The same Christ who died for their sins and was resurrected for them, is the same Christ who has died for our sins and was resurrected for us.

Concerning hope, St. Augustine the third century Bishop of Hippo said that *"Hope has two beautiful daughters; their names are Anger and Courage. Anger at the way things are, and Courage to see that they do not remain as they are."*

Therefore, we have a hope that's alive. It's a hope that's not dead, or stale or stagnant. It's a hope that's not dormant or latent. It's a hope that's not dull, drab or dreary.

Ours is a hope that's alive. What does a hope that's alive really look like? Martin Luther King, Jr. stated that hope is always animated by our faith and love. He further reminded us that hope is the refusal to give up despite insurmountable odds. He intimated that if we have hope, you have faith in something.

What does a hope that's alive look like?
Hope reminds us that God is not finished with any of us yet.
Hope insists that greater is God who is us, than he who is in the world.
Hope says that we can do all things through Christ who strengthens us.
Hope helps us to know that we may not know what tomorrow holds, but we know who holds tomorrow.

What does a hope that's alive really look like?
Hope woke us up this morning...
Hope started us on our way...
Hope put food on the table... clothes on our backs...
        and clothed us in our right minds.

Hope healed the sick.
Hope raised the dead.
Hope took two fish and five loaves of bread, and fed more than five thousand hungry people.
Hope delivers... hope saves... hope redeems us.

Our hope is in Jesus the Christ who was resurrected on the third day! We've got a hope that is alive!

20 - OUT OF MOUNTAINS OF DESPAIR –
MARTIN LUTHER KING, JR. AND HOPE
(An Essay)

In one of his later sermons, "The Meaning of Hope," Martin Luther King, Jr. in 1967, defined hope as that quality which is "necessary for life."[22] He asserted that hope is to be viewed as "animated and undergirded by faith and love." In his mind, if you had hope, you had faith in something. Thus, hope shares the belief that "all reality hinges on moral foundations."[23] For King, hope was the refusal to give up "despite overwhelming odds." It beckons us to love everybody – both our allies and enemies. It helps us to see that we can resist giving up on one another because our lives together are animated by the belief that God is present in each and every one of us, and in every circumstance.

King, Hope and the American Dream

Today, many people would agree that a great deal of progress has been made in light of King's dream of equality and his call to action over the course of his 14-year public ministry. With the passage of the Civil Rights Act in 1964, and Voting Rights Act and Immigration and Nationality Act in 1965

---

[22] Martin Luther King, Jr., "The Meaning of Hope," sermon delivered on December 10, 1967; Martin Luther King, Jr. King Center Archives, Atlanta, GA, 5ff. See also Baker-Fletcher, *Somebodyness,* 132.
[23] King, "The Meaning of Hope".

respectively, greater opportunities for many women and persons of color in our society, the election in 2008 of Barack Hussein Obama as the first American president of African descent, and expanding engagement of persons across cultures and classes, we have seen concrete evidence of the movement toward King's dream which was most clearly and demonstratively expressed during his August 1963 "I Have a Dream" speech at the March on Washington for Jobs and Freedom.

These are days of tremendous change and challenge. From the collapse of economies that affect most people – to wars that are now being fought around the world – to the proliferation of violence that affects many people and communities - to the healthcare crisis that results in millions of Americans still living without affordable, adequate, accessible healthcare – to the ever-expanding prison industrial complex, mass incarceration, and over-incarceration of Black and Brown people, where we are reminded by Michelle Alexander in her book, *The New Jim Crow* that we have more Black and Brown men in prison than we do in college - indeed, these are days of unprecedented change and challenge.

Perhaps, the most glaring signs of social distress in America today can be found in the lingering problem of racism. It is clear that race continues to matter in America, and that we are not yet at the place of being post-racial or post-racist in the churches or society. Michael Eric Dyson addresses this matter in his book, *Can You Hear Me Now?,* where he insists that the critical question that is before society today is not if we are yet a *post-racial* society, and the question is not even if we should strive to become post-racial, but the critical question is how might we move closer towards becoming a *post-racist* society?

Indeed, there are considerable challenges to arriving at a hope that is yet to be fully realized. In 1992, philosopher Cornel West authored an important book entitled, *Race Matters*. The book was written against the backdrop of the Los Angeles riots of April 1992, which followed the acquittal of the police officers charged in the beating of Rodney King, and the ensuing racial tensions in that city. In the book, West pointed to what he referred to as the "nihilism of Black America" – where a certain nothingness, meaninglessness, lovelessness and hopelessness seemed to have pervaded and permeated much of our society – particularly in urban contexts, and as it pertains to Black and Brown people. According to him at that time, race mattered in America, and thus we as a society must continue to attend to matters of race.

In light of these realities, realizing hope is not easy. In his 2008 book, *Hope on a Tightrope*, West laid the groundwork for a discourse on hope in its contemporary context. He cautioned against a false sense of security in hope, yet unborn. He posited that real hope is grounded in a particularly messy struggle and it can be betrayed by naive projections of a better future that ignores the necessity of doing real work. For West, real hope is closely connected to attributes like courage, faith, freedom and wisdom. It comes out of a history of struggle, and points to a future filled with the possibilities of promise and progress.[24]

One of the things that Martin Luther King, Jr. intimated in his 1963 "I Have a Dream" speech was a hope that God would "hew out of the mountain of despair, a stone of hope."

---

[24] Cornel West, Hope *on a Tightrope* (New York: Smiley Books, 2008), 6.

The despair that King alluded to then was capsulated in what he deemed to be the "triplets of evil" – racism, poverty (classism) and war (militarism). In King's estimation, these were the major categories of the social dis-ease that afflicted America then, and thus there was the need for the struggle for civil rights, human rights and equal rights, and thus also a need for the March on Washington for Jobs and Freedom, the Poor People's Campaign, opposition to the War in Vietnam, and a renewed call/commitment to prophetic action.

As King spoke at the Lincoln Memorial on that sunlit day in August 1963, he shared with the crowd, the nation and the world a compelling dream – a vision of the *Beloved Community* - of a world where every "child would be judged not by the color of their skin, but by the content of their character." He articulated a hope that America would live up to the true meaning of its creed as found in the Declaration of Independence, "We hold these truths to be self-evident, that all (people) are created equal."

A part of the moral prerogative of churches, civil and human rights organizations, and all other institutions and persons concerned about the common good and well-being of the world today remains that of speaking truthfully and hopefully to the critical moral and social issues of the contemporary age, and then working to bring about progressive change. The task ahead is to help devise and articulate a framework for engaging in critical and constructive advocacy for the disinherited among us – the poor, violated, marginalized, suffering and oppressed.

And an important aspect of the churches' prophetic task is also to be introspective and self-critical as it pertains to issues such as the proliferation of the prosperity gospel, the lack of activism in many circles, the inability or unwillingness of the churches today to speak and act prophetically on matters of contemporary concern such as war, domestic terror and gun violence, the widening gap between the rich and the poor in America and around the world, the ongoing proliferation of racial (and other forms of) bigotry, the marginalization of too many in our society, along with the generally violent and misogynistic nature of hip hop and other expressions of popular culture.

Barack Obama and Hope Renewed

At the historic election of Barack H. Obama as the 44th President of the United States on November 11, 2008, many people seemed to sense (and hope) that his election had ushered in an age of post-racism and post-racialism in America – and perhaps around the world.

In his 2006 book, *The Audacity of Hope*, then-Senator Barack Obama offered words of caution to America in thinking that we may have arrived at becoming "post-racial" or that we already live in a color-blind society, and that we are beyond the need for discourse and critical engagement as it regards race, racism and related forms of oppression and injustice. He wrote:

> To say that we are one people is not to suggest that race no longer matters – that the fight for equality has been won, or that the problems that minorities face in this country today are largely self-inflicted. We know the statistics: On almost every single socioeconomic indicator, from infant mortality to life expectancy to

employment to home ownership, black and Latino Americans in particular lag far behind their white counterparts.[25]

In a major address prior to his election entitled "A More Perfect Union", delivered on March 18, 2008 during his presidential campaign, Obama offered an analysis of the prevalence of racial tensions which have continued to define the relationship between the black and white communities in America. Obama asserted that to simply shelve anger or "wish away" the race problem in America could prove to be seriously detrimental. Unambiguously, he pointed to a belief that race factors into the opportunities provided to each American citizen.

To support his assertion, he noted that inferior school systems today are often the ones that were segregated fifty years ago. He further asserted that the history of racism in America is undeniably at the root of the lack of opportunities for African Americans today. In light of this, it is necessary for all Americans to unite and battle racial prejudices and oppression. According to Obama, in order to move to a "more perfect union", people of all races need to recognize the historically oppressive and tyrannical nature of racism and its impact on the black experience in America.

A good deal of the political discourse during the 2008 presidential primaries focused on then-Senator Barack Obama's membership at Trinity United Church of Christ in Chicago, and

---

[25] Barack Obama, *The Audacity of Hope: Thoughts on Reclaiming the American Dream* (New York: Three Rivers Press, 2006), 232.

his 20-year relationship with Rev. Dr. Jeremiah Wright, the church's pastor at that time. On the surface, many of the concerns levied against Obama in light of his relationship with Wright centered on comments that Wright had made in several sermons in which he offered pointed, and what some considered to have been derogatory critiques of America and the Bush presidential administration in the aftermath of the 2001 terrorist attacks and in light of the then war in Iraq.

In light of Wright's role as a prophetic leader in the church, community and across the nation for over thirty years, perhaps then it is not coincidental that like him, who in 2007 expressed his opposition to the war in Iraq, Martin Luther King, Jr., (40 years prior) on April 4, 1967 at Riverside Church in New York City – in a sermon entitled, "Beyond Vietnam – A Time to Break Silence" – similarly expressed in vehement terms his opposition to the war in Vietnam.[26] King stated:

> At this point I should make it clear that while I have tried in these last few minutes to give a voice to the voiceless on Vietnam and to understand the arguments of those who are called enemy, I am as deeply concerned about our troops there as anything else. For it occurs to me that what we are submitting them to in Vietnam is not simply the brutalizing process that goes on in any war where armies face each other and seek to destroy. We are adding cynicism to the process of death, for they must know after a short period there that

---

[26] Martin Luther King, Jr., "Beyond Vietnam – A Time to Break Silence, in *A Testament of Hope: The Essential Writings and Speeches of Martin Luther King, Jr.,* James Melvin Washington, ed. (New York: Harper Collins, 1986), 238.

none of the things we claim to be fighting for are really involved.

King continued:

> Somehow this madness must cease. We must stop now. I speak as a child of God and brother of the suffering poor of Vietnam. I speak for those whose land is being laid waste, whose homes are being destroyed, whose culture is being subverted. I speak for the poor of America who are paying the double price of smashed hopes at home and death corruption in Vietnam.[27]

In a speech at the University of Michigan in 1962, King shared a point that he would make on several other subsequent occasions. He pointed out that we are faced with a choice in our life together, and that we will either learn to live together as (sisters and brothers), or perish together as fools.[28]

Finding Hope amidst Despair

In many ways, America is a contradiction laying in the metaphysical conundrum of hope and despair – with wealth and poverty, abundance and scarcity, and the quest for truth amidst untruth being simultaneously extant. In the wealthiest nation in the world, with abundance across many sectors, income and wealth disparity among the richest and the rest of Americans is

---

[27] King, "Beyond Vietnam – A Time to Break Silence", 238.
[28] Martin Luther King, Jr. This statement was in a speech at the University of Michigan, Ann Arbor, Michigan in 1962. King would make this assertion on several subsequent occasions.

most evident in the plight of the poorest Americans – those who are housing and food insecure, with related forms of scarcity in adequate healthcare, nutrition, clean water, education, employment, safety, technology and transportation. Mohandas Gandhi intimated years ago that "poverty is the worst form of violence."

Howard Thurman, in "Through the Coming Year" offered a confessional prayer that captures the nature of the existential despair that we all may struggle with in seeking to do God's will –

In my confusion I shall often say
the word that is not true
and do the thing of which I am ashamed.
There will be errors in the mind
and great inaccuracies of judgment.

In seeking the light,
I shall again and again find myself
walking in the darkness.[29]

Today, I propose that we live within the crucible of *Ten Contemporary Social Plagues*: (1) Poverty, income/wealth inequality and inequity; (2) Racism and xenophobia; (3) Misogyny and violence against women, and lack of comparable worth; (4) Lack of full attention to the environment, global warming and climate change; (5) Under-education and miseducation of large segments of society; (6) Financial profiteering of the gun lobby, and gun violence; (7) The

---

[29] Howard Thurman, *Meditations of the Heart* (Richmond, IN: Friends United Press, 1976), 96.

growing prison industrial complex, financial profiteering on incarceration, and the over-incarceration of Black and Brown people; (8) Anti-immigration and immigrant bashing; (9) Police brutality; and (10) Militarism and terrorism (domestic and foreign).[30]

These ten contemporary social plagues tend to make hope fleeting. Yet, amidst despair, hope beckons the churches and society to proactively and prophetically act to address the plight of those who have the least among us – many Black and Brown persons, our homeless and hungry neighbors, and those of our siblings who are immigrants - and to see poverty as in and of itself, inflicting violence upon its victims – violence which stains the soul and dignity of persons, violence which affects persons' physical well-being and threatens their lives, and violence which impacts the potential and possibility of individuals and society as a whole.

Some of what underlies our will to such violence on the soul, and our inability and/or unwillingness to address it is rooted, again, in the very real and deep racial and class divides that exist among us. Ta-Nehisi Coates in his book, *Between the World and Me*, writes about growing up on the streets of Baltimore, and states that "race is the child of racism, not the father."[31] By extension it could be argued that class (and caste) is the child of classism, not the mother. The concomitant evils of racism and classism serve as severe detriments to bringing about wholeness for those among us who find ourselves living

---

[30] C. Anthony Hunt, in *The Beloved Community Toolkit* (Bel Air, MD: C. Anthony Hunt, 2018).
[31] Ta-Nehisi Coates, *Between the World and Me* (New York: Spiegel and Grau, 2015), 7.

on the margins of society, and these evils are ultimately detrimental to the realization of the *Beloved Community.*

Our divine and moral imperative, amidst such existential despair, is to speak out and act out – individually and collectively – with and for our neighbors - to speak out and act out with compassion and justice. Our divine and moral imperative is to speak out and act out in ways that address the immediate needs of God's people who must endure existential despair by providing adequate shelter, food, clean water, clothing, healthcare and safety – while also addressing the serious systemic and structural political, economic and moral concerns that lead us to ask why our sisters and brothers are forced to endure such existential despair in the first place.

With all that continues to plague America and the world, there's the need to renew our commitment to Martin Luther King, Jr.'s dream, and to heed a call to action. Where might hope reside in and among us as we look to the future? King stated that "The hopeless individual is the dead individual." In his view, hope had a transformative quality that keeps human beings "alive" both spiritually and psychologically.[32] Hope, therefore, is "one of the basic structures of an adequate life."

In the third century, Augustine, the Bishop of Hippo is attributed with intimating that *"Hope has two beautiful daughters; their names are Anger and Courage. Anger at the way things are, and Courage to see that they do not remain the way they are."* Hope does not settle for the status quo – whatever it is – but always pushes towards a better future.

---

[32] King, "The Meaning of Hope", 5. See also, Baker-Fletcher, *Somebodyness,* 132.

In *A Theology of Hope,* Jürgen Moltmann intimated that:

> "Hope alone is to be called 'realistic', because it alone takes seriously the possibilities with which all reality is fraught. It does not take things as they happen to stand or to lie, but as progressing, moving things with possibilities of change. Only as long as the world and the people in it are in a fragmented and experimental state which is not yet resolved, is there any sense in earthly hopes."[33]

Moltmann posits an eschatologically-centered perspective on hope that focuses on the hope that Christ's Resurrection brings. For him, the hope of the Christian faith is hope in the resurrection of Christ crucified. Accordingly, through faith we are bound to Christ, and as such we have the hope of the resurrected Christ, and can anticipate his return. Hope and faith, Moltmann posits, depend on each other to remain true and substantial; and only with both may one find "not only a consolation in suffering, but also the protest of the divine promise against suffering."[34]

Hope strengthens faith, helps believers live lives of love, and directs persons toward a new creation of all things. It creates in us a "passion for the possible." As Moltmann asserts, "For our knowledge and comprehension of reality, and our reflections on it, that means at least this: that in the medium of hope our theological concepts become not judgments which nail

---

[33] Jürgen Moltmann, *A Theology of Hope* (Minneapolis, MN: Fortress, 1993), 25.
[34] Moltmann, pp. 19-20.

reality down to what it is, but anticipations which show reality its prospects and its future possibilities."[35]

King framed his vision of hope within the context of the *Beloved Community*. Hope can be found in the possibilities that we will continue to discover ways to capitalize on those experiences and encounters that will lead to us being intentional, authentic and radically inclusive community. Hope for a better future is rooted and grounded in our shared potential and commitment to change the world for the better. The church and society today look quite different from the church and society of fifty years ago. Progress can be seen in many areas. And yet there is still much work that lies ahead of us. This is the hope that must be realized if the church is to be the church, the *Beloved Community*, that King imagined, and which Christ calls it to become.

Is There No Balm?

The prophet Jeremiah offered a vision of hope for a people experiencing despair and exile in a strange land. In the sixth century B.C.E., the Israelites were in Babylon – alienated from their land, from their God, and – many of them - from their loved ones.

We can imagine that the Israelites experienced what Friedrich Nietzsche, Cornel West and other philosophers have come to refer to as an apparent nihilism – an apparent nothingness, meaninglessness, lovelessness and hopelessness that can come to define the existence of a people amidst such

---

[35] Moltmann, 22

despair. In Psalm 137, while in Babylonian exile, the Israelites expressed their anguish:

> *By the rivers of Babylon, we sat and wept*
> *   when we remembered Zion.*
> *There on the poplars*
> *   we hung our harps,*
> *for there our captors asked us for songs,*
> *   our tormentors demanded songs of joy;*
> *   they said, "Sing us one of the songs of Zion!"*
> *How can we sing the songs of the Lord*
> *   while in a foreign land? (Psalm 137:1-4)*

It was against this backdrop of the apparent existential nihilism of the Israelites in Babylon that Jeremiah shared these words of hope:

> *"For surely, I know the plans I have for you, says the Lord, plans for your welfare (shalom, wholeness, well-being), and not for your harm, plans to give you a future with hope." (Jeremiah 29:11)*

On numerous occasions, Martin Luther King, Jr. pointed out that the nature of hope is evident in questions posed by the prophet Jeremiah –

> *"Is there no balm in Gilead; is there no physician there? Why then has the health of my poor people not been restored?"* (Jeremiah 8:22)

King intimated that amidst the oppression that many black people had experienced in America – through slavery, Jim Crow and persistent racism - people of faith in God were able to convert the *question marks* of the prophet Jeremiah's lament, into *exclamation points* as they affirmed their faith and proclaimed hope in the living and life-giving God, in a song. And so, they sang in affirmation of their faith, with blessed assurance:

> *There is a balm in Gilead,*
> *to make the wounded whole*
> *There is a balm in Gilead,*
> *To heal the sin-sick soul.*
> *Sometimes I feel discouraged,*
> *And think my work's in vain.*
> *And then the Holy Spirit*
> *Revives my soul again!* [36]

King's ultimate hope rested in the prospects that the "World House" – *the Beloved Community* – would someday be realized. He stated in *Where Do We Go from Here?* that, "Our hope for creative living in this "World House" that we have inherited lies in our ability to reestablish the moral ends of our lives in personal character and social justice. Without this spiritual and moral reawakening, we shall destroy ourselves in the misuse of our own instruments."[37]

---

[36] *Songs of Zion: Supplemental Worship Resources* (Nashville: Abingdon Press, 1981), 123.

[37] King, *Where Do We Go from Here?*, see also Cornel West, ed., *The Radical King: Martin Luther King, Jr.* (Boston: Beacon Press, 2015), 80.

In the final analysis, for King, the realization of the *Beloved Community* depends on never giving up hoping amidst despair. Indeed, today, he might affirm the encouraging sentiments of the great poet Langston Hughes to –

Hold fast to dreams,
For when dreams die,
Life is a broken winged bird
That cannot fly.

Hold fast to dreams,
For when dreams go,
Life is a barren field
Frozen with snow.

21 - KEEP HOPING (A Sermon)

In you, Lord my God, I put my trust. I trust in you; do not let me be put to shame, nor let my enemies triumph over me. No one who hopes in you will ever be put to shame, but shame will come on those who are treacherous without cause. Show me your ways, Lord, teach me your paths. Guide me in your truth and teach me, for you are God my Savior, and my hope is in you all day long. (Psalm 25:1-5)

Near the end of his life, Rev. Dr. Martin Luther King, Jr. published a book entitled, *Where Do We Go from Here: Chaos or Community?* In it, he reiterated a point he had made on several other occasions. He pointed out that we are faced with a choice in our life together, and that we will either learn to live together as brothers and sisters, or we will die together as fools.

A part of the moral prerogative of churches, civil and human rights organizations and all other institutions and persons concerned about the well-being of our world today remains that of speaking to the critical moral and social issues of the contemporary age. It is our task to help articulate a framework for engaging in critical and constructive advocacy for the disinherited among us – the poor, the violated and the oppressed.

In light of this, where might hope reside among us as we look to the future? King framed his vision of hope within the context of the *Beloved Community*. In one of his later sermons,

"The Meaning of Hope," he defined hope as that quality which is "necessary for life."[38]

King asserted that hope was to be viewed as "animated and undergirded by faith and love." In his mind, if you had hope, you had faith in something. For King, hope was the refusal to give up "despite overwhelming odds." In his famous "I Have a Dream" speech delivered on the steps of the Lincoln Memorial in Washington, DC on August 28, 1963, King shared that a part of his dream was that we would be able *"to hew out of the mountain of despair, a stone of hope."*

With all that is going on in our world today, some would assert that it becomes difficult to locate God, and recognize what God is doing, what God is up to in our lives, and in the world. With all the noise and confusion in the atmosphere, it's often difficult to hear from the Lord.

Some would argue that we are living in a time where in no small way there's a paucity of hope. There's a paucity of hope - where a certain nihilism - a certain emptiness, lovelessness, lifelessness, nothingness, meaninglessness - and indeed a certain hopelessness pervades and permeates the church and the world.

The great neo-Soul singer India Arie alluded to this in her song - *There's Hope.*

> *Gas prices - they just keep on rising (There's hope)*
> *The government - they keep on lying*
> *But we gotta keep on surviving...*

---

[38] King, sermon delivered on December 10, 1967, see Garth Baker-Fletcher, *Somebodyness: Martin Luther King, Jr. and the Theory of Dignity,* 132.

Keep living our truth and do the best we can do.

I know somebody is saying "I hear you India. I know what you're talking about when you say, despite all that's going on, "we gotta keep on surviving." I hear you India, but if you know like I know sometimes hope seems like it's on a tight rope." Hope sometimes seems hard to see. Hope sometimes seems hard to hold onto, and it's difficult to hang in.

What we need to remember is that we're not the first people to be living and surviving in a paucity of hope. The people in the world just prior to Jesus's birth were living in a similar state.

From Malachi to Matthew, the Bible shows us that hope had been silent for over 400 years. The people of the Lord's day had waited, and waited on God. They had waited on the Lord, and *all they could do was to keep on surviving – all they could do was keep hoping.*

Listen to the psalmist as he sings in Psalm 25. He's singing the song of a people whose hope was on a tightrope. He's singing the song of a people who had gone through attacks by their enemies.

Hear the psalmist's lyrics – *"In you, Lord my God, I put my trust. I trust in you; do not let me be put to shame, nor let my enemies triumph over me. No one who hopes in you will ever be put to shame, but shame will come on those who are treacherous without cause".*

What is it that can help us to keep hoping in times like these? In whom can we hope?

The psalmist ended his song by declaring that *"my hope is in you, God, all day long."* We are likewise beckoned to place our hope, to place our future, in God's hands.

In Jeremiah 29:11, the prophet offered a vision of hope for a people experiencing exile in a strange city. Here, the Israelites were in Babylon – alienated from their land, alienated from their God, and alienated – many of them - from their loved ones. It is against this backdrop of near hopelessness that Jeremiah shared these words of hope:

> "For surely, I know the plans I have for you, says the Lord, plans for your welfare (shalom, wholeness), and not for your harm, plans to give you a future with hope."

Those were the same times that would lead Jeremiah earlier to offer provocative questions to the same people –

> "Is there no balm in Gilead? Is there no healing there? Why then has the health of my people not been restored?" (Jer. 8:22)

In reflecting on this text from Jeremiah, Martin Luther King, Jr. pointed out that the evidence of faith and hope is found in the fact that Blacks who were enslaved and oppressed in America were able to convert the *question mark* of the prophet Jeremiah's lament, into an *exclamation point* as they affirmed their faith and hope in the living and life-giving God in a song:

> *There is a balm in Gilead,*
> *To make the wounded whole*
> *There is a balm in Gilead,*
> *To heal the sin-sick soul.*
> *Sometimes I feel discouraged*

And think my work's in vain.
And then the Holy Spirit
Revives my soul again![39]

Hope beckons us to love everybody – both our allies and enemies. Hope helps us to see that we can resist giving up on one another because our lives together are animated by the belief that God is present in each and every one of us. Hope helps us to believe that God is the orchestrator of mercy and justice for all people.

Hope can be found in the possibilities that we will continue to discover ways to capitalize on those experiences and encounters that will lead to us being intentional and inclusive community. This is the hope that must be realized if we are to be the *Beloved Community* that Martin Luther King, Jr. imagined, and that God wills.

In the days ahead, may we continue to conjure the audacity to dream dreams and see visions, and may we have the temerity to hope against all that seems to rise and push against hope. May we have the courage to hold onto hope.

---

[39] See *Songs of Zion*, 123.

22 - A PRAYER FOR COURAGE
(by Ted Loder in "My Heart in My Mouth: Prayers for our Lives")

God of grace,

as you did with Rosa Parks and Martin Luther King, Jr.,

Mother Teresa, Nelson Mandela and Desmond Tutu,

strengthen us to answer with brave hearts

your call to help shape a world

not of death and oppression,

but of life and hope.

23 - GOT HOPE! (A Sermon)

(This sermon was first delivered at Epworth Chapel UMC, Baltimore in April 2015 in the aftermath of the police-involved death of Freddie Gray, and then as the keynote address in May 2015 at the international meeting of the Association of United Methodist Chancellors in Baltimore, MD in May 2015.)

"...and we boast in our hope of sharing the glory of God... knowing that our suffering produces endurance, and endurance produces character, and character produces hope, and hope does not disappoint us..." **Romans 5:1-5**

This week has been filled with tumult and turmoil just in our backyard. We've experienced the very public funeral of Mr. Freddie Gray. We've witnessed the lashing out of many of our young people - and some not so young people - some of whom have expressed their anger, frustration and outrage by rioting and looting at Mondawmin Mall – just a few miles from us.

We've witnessed looting and destruction of several drug stores and food markets – destruction and burning of houses, cars and church property. We've witnessed lashing out with violence against police officers. We've seen the presence of the Maryland National Guard planted down in the city to maintain order on the streets.

We've witnessed a city-wide curfew, and we've witnessed numerous people arrested. And amidst all of this, there were at least five more people murdered in Baltimore, and at least 12 more shot this past week – one of those murdered being a close friend of the late Mr. Freddie Gray. We've seen city and state officials wrestle with what would be the best course of action to bring about peace and a sense of justice for Mr. Gray's family, for Sandtown-Winchester, for zip-code 21217, and for the city of Baltimore.

The eyes of the entire nation and world have been turned on Baltimore. We've seen and experienced what has appeared to be hopelessness, and what can happen when some people among us feel hopeless and unheard. Dr. Martin Luther King, Jr. intimated that riots are the language of the unheard.

And in the midst of all of this – we have also seen many people come together to pray for peace and justice. We've seen people come together to march in peaceful protest. We've seen people come together to work to rebuild Baltimore, a city torn by decades of destruction. We've seen churches open their doors to feed the hungry, and provide safe haven for children. We've seen some people celebrate at the announcement that criminal charges would be brought against those involved in the death of Mr. Gray.

We have seen the Baltimore Symphony Orchestra leave their music halls in the midst of the rioting to offer beautiful music on the streets of the city. We've seen phenomenal acts of generosity and kindness. So, in the midst of all that we've gone through this past week – through it all – we realize that we've still got hope.

The days, times and conditions in which the apostle Paul ministered were probably in many ways not unlike what we are experiencing today. In Rome, there was an apparent paucity of hope – even among the people who had come to know of the living Christ. An apparent paucity of hope is what Paul was preaching to here – maybe due to the existence of severe persecution of the people in the church because of their beliefs in Christ, and maybe also because of the very real challenges that they faced in their daily living.

In many ways, the church today is well-acquainted with those realities, both within and outside the church, that challenge our hopefulness. Indeed, an inventory of our world and the church gives clear indication that we teeter on the brink of hopelessness and despair – with wars that have lasted far too long and killed way too many, violence in too many of our neighborhoods, increasing gaps between the "have-gots" and the "have-nots", and matters that threaten to divide the churches and our communities. We teeter on the brink of hopelessness.

And yet, if the church has been, and is to be anything, we are to be a people who boldly embodies hope. This was Paul's very point in his words to the Christians in Rome – *"...and we boast in our hope of sharing the glory of God... knowing that our suffering produces endurance, and endurance produces character, and character produces hope, and hope does not disappoint us..."*

Hope is real, and should be real to you and me. Hope is what the great German theologian Jurgen Moltmann, in *A Theology of Hope,* wrote about when he wrote – "Hope alone is to be called "realistic" because it alone takes seriously the possibilities with which all reality is fraught. Hope does not take things as they happen to stand or to lie, but as progressing, moving things with possibilities of change."

King in "The Meaning of Hope" defined Christian hope as that quality which is "necessary for life.' King asserted that hope is to be viewed as "animated and under girded by faith and love." In his mind, if you had hope, you had faith in something.

Thus, for him, hope shares the belief that "all reality hinges on moral foundations." It was, for King, the refusal to give up "despite overwhelming odds."

Hope assures us that justice will come… that peace will come…. and that change is going to come.

We've got hope! One of the things I've learned about hope is that there are times when we tend to trivialize and even mythicize hope so much so that we often don't recognize it even when it is in our midst. I say this to suggest that if we take time to look around, we will see hope all around us.

Children laughing and playing, that's hope. Music in our ears, that's hope. Food on our tables, that's hope. Clothes on our backs, that's hope. Shoes on our feet, that's hope. New awakenings and new beginnings, that's hope!

And so, whatever our lot today, as people in and of Christ, we've got hope! And let me remind us what hope really is. Our hope is in the name of Jesus. Hope lets us wake up knowing that *"morning by morning new mercies I see"* (Lamentations 3:23). Hope lets us lie down at night knowing that *"weeping may endure for a night, but joy comes in the morning"* (Psalm 30:5). Hope reminds us that *"faith is the substance of things hoped for, and the evidence of things not seen"* (Hebrews 11:1).

Hope is what Rev. Charles Albert Tindley knew about when he wrote -
"I do not know how long 'twill be
Or what the future holds for (you or) me
But this I know
If Jesus leads (us),
We'll get home, someday…"

We've Got Hope!

24 - *FREDDIE GRAY, THE POLICE AND THE LANGUAGE OF THE UNHEARD (An Essay)*

(This reflection was written on April 12, 2020 at the five-year anniversary of the arrest and subsequent death of Mr. Freddie Gray while in police custody in Baltimore, Maryland.)

Today marks the five-year anniversary of the arrest of Mr. Freddie Gray, the 25-year-old man who would die a week later on April 19, 2015 while in police custody in Baltimore. While media pundits, prognosticators and political opportunists directed their attention on Baltimore over the following few days, and have continued to do so over the past few years, a few things may help place into perspective what happened following Mr. Gray's death.

First, a question that many people have asked over the five years since the uprisings (riots) in Baltimore which started on April 26, 2015, in the aftermath of Mr. Gray's death is "what's changed in Baltimore?" I suggest that the answer is that not much has shifted in terms of the socio-political and economic landscape in the city. To-date, there have been over 1500 murders in Baltimore since Freddie Gray's death, public schools continue to be underfunded and are generally underperforming, and poverty persists in large swaths of the city, particularly in the eastern, western and southern corridors.

Five years ago, at Mr. Gray's death, I wrote that one of the things I learned in my training as an economist, and something that continues to stick with me, is to always follow the money (resources), and/or the lack thereof. In many ways,

Baltimore - like many American cities - continues to be "the tale of two cities" – one among the rich and the other among the rest of everybody else. Economic inequality, poverty and educational disparities are the root causes of what continues to plague cities like Baltimore. And Mohandas Gandhi's sentiments still ring true - "Poverty is the worst form of violence."

Second, no one was found to have been responsible for Freddie Gray's death. While the wheels of justice began to turn, and trials were scheduled for the six police officers charged in Mr. Gray's death, none of the six who either arrested, drove or detained Gray were found to be responsible.

Third, in the five years since Freddie Gray's death, again, there have been over 1500 killings in Baltimore, which continues to make it one of the most violent cities in America, and in-fact, the world. The vast majority of those who have been murdered are young black men (under 35). And while there have been several instances of police violence directed towards citizens during this time, the vast majority of those murdered in Baltimore in the last five years have been the result of fratricide - Blacks killing other Blacks.

Fourth, while several grassroots organizations emerged in Baltimore in the aftermath of Freddie Gray's death that raised their voices, expended a great amount of energy, and sought to make substantive changes on the ground, many did not stay to sustain their efforts, and the systemic socio-economic conditions that were correlative, if not causal, to Gray's death - poverty, miseducation, poor housing and homelessness, drug and alcohol addiction, under- and unemployment, lack of adequate transportation systems, inadequate healthcare, poor nutrition, environmental injustice, etc. - remain extant. While many people, both within and outside the city, have talked about the need for change, little has actually changed in communities like Sandtown-Winchester where Freddie Gray was born, raised, educated and arrested.

Fifth, again, while none of the six police officers charged in Freddie Gray's death were found to be responsible, the Baltimore City Police Department now remains under a federal consent decree because of ongoing patterns of inappropriate and illegal activity across several Baltimore City Police Department agencies.

In addition to justice for Freddie Gray and his family, complete justice would include a strategic/concrete plan involving all parties in Baltimore and the state of Maryland (politicians, businesses, religious and community leaders) aimed at addressing all political/economic disparities in communities across the city, like Sandtown-Winchester - disparities in the areas of education, employment, housing, health-care, policing (safety), transportation and technology. To deal with the Freddie Gray case only, and to then continue with business as usual in Baltimore would serve as a mere smokescreen, and would result in history continuing to repeat itself.

As we remember the life of Mr. Freddie Gray and others around the nation who have died while in police custody, my hope and prayer remains that those in elective and appointive office – locally and nationally - who are charged with providing leadership would direct their attention to the people of our nation's cities - like Baltimore, Chicago, New York, St. Louis, Flint and New Orleans - and seek to devise real, substantive, systemic, strategic solutions to our cities' challenges.

25 - *CHARLOTTESVILLE AND AMERICAN RACISM TODAY (An Essay)*

The events that transpired in Charlottesville, Virginia during the second weekend of August 2017 are a clear emblem of social disembodiment in America today. These events were not surprising to many people familiar with the history, and acquainted with the legacy of racism in America. As young white men wielded torches through a college town, the home of the University of Virginia - the school founded by one of America's founding fathers, Thomas Jefferson - and chanted anti-Semitic and racist slogans, the truth that was revealed over the course of that weekend is that the so-called alt-right, white supremacy, white nationalism and neo-Nazism is alive in America.

Having traveled Virginia Highway 29 all of my life from Washington, D.C. to Lynchburg, Virginia to visit my extended family, I have passed through Charlottesville, and ridden past the University of Virginia campus dozens of times. It has always been, and continues to be my impression that in the rural communities surrounding Charlottesville and the University of Virginia, non-white people are not always welcome, and racist elements have existed over the years, and do so today.

In the words of Malcolm X, "the chickens came home to roost" in Charlottesville in August 2017. What occurred there did not happen coincidentally or by accident, but is the offspring of over a decade of a breeding politics of race, division, hate and fear in America that has become much more pronounced and vitriolic, and at points, violent in the last few years. Indeed, Charlottesville confirmed again that *'racism is the elephant in America's living room'*.

The very nature of racism is that it is rooted in hatred. There's no conceivable way in space and time (metaphysically) that love and hate can co-exist. The two cannot occupy the same space and time. Racism and white supremacy, in any of its forms, is rooted in hatred, and those who are racists do not and cannot love those whom they deem to be racially inferior.

What happened in Charlottesville was also a reminder that history is the parent of the present and future. Alabama and Virginia are the homes of Jefferson Davis and the Confederacy. If Alabama is the cradle of the Confederacy, then Virginia is its second seed-bed.

It is interesting then that things came to greater light as to the ongoing race problem in America in Charlottesville against the backdrop of not only the legacies of Confederate general Robert E. Lee and Confederate president Jefferson Davis, but against the backdrop of the oppressive and complex legacy of Thomas Jefferson, Montebello, Sally Hemings, and Jefferson's "Notes on the State of Virginia" (1785), in which, based on his Enlightenment Theory of race and sub-humanity, Jefferson questioned the requisite abilities of Black and Native American (non-white) persons to reason.

Some who defended the events in Charlottesville, and the actions of the Proud Boys and others argued that the symbols which were the focal points of the weekend's events – confederate monuments and flags – have little, if any, real meaning and connection to what is going on in contemporary America. But as Paul Tillich expounded upon in his *Systematic Theology II*, the very nature of symbols is that they invariably have meaning attached to them. The same symbol could mean different things to different people, but they have meaning.

Whatever one's perspective, in America, the hundreds of remaining Confederate monuments (some of which were the focal point of events in Charlottesville), the thousands of Confederate flags spread across America, the visible display of swastikas, people parading in public in white robes and hoods, images of torches, lynching trees, strange fruit, faces at bottoms of wells, and churches burning and being bombed mean something to each of us within the context of the past, present and future of the nation.

A large part of the ongoing legacy of the display of Confederate monuments and other related symbols across the land (in the South and North), and the pain attached to them for many Americans, has to be understood against the backdrop of the terrible atrocities - the concomitant suffering and death - of the American slave trade, which lasted for 246 years, and the ensuing years of politics of nullification and redemption, and Jim Crow. There's no historically valid way to detach the American slave trade from the rise of the Confederacy in the 19th century, the politics of redemption and nullification of the Black Reconstruction, and Jim Crow through the 20th century, with the rise of the Ku Klux Klan and white citizens councils, and Charlottesville today. For many people, these Confederate monuments and symbols point to the condoning, celebrating, and honoring of division and hatred, and minimizing and denying of the dehumanizing realities and effects of slavery in America, the likes of which has not occurred at any other time or place in the civilized world.

What transpired in Charlottesville in 2017 also shed light on the fact that the faces of domestic terrorism and neo-Nazism in America today are in large measure young white males who have perpetrated mass murder - like Dylann Roof, Sean Urbanski and James Alex Fields, among others. And while some of America's national leadership has continued to work at revising and pushing immigration policies designed to keep entire classes of people out of the nation based on their religion and/or nationality (e.g. Muslims, Syrians, Mexicans and Central Americans), devising policies to build border walls and separate children from their immigrant parents, and revising policies allowing for the building of more privately owned prison facilities that will disproportionately house Black and Brown people, thus perpetuating what Michelle Alexander refers to as the "New Jim Crow" in America - the uncomfortable truth reiterated with the events in Charlottesville, and the shoes that continue to hurt America's feet as a nation is that racism remains an extant - living, breathing and breeding - reality around many dinner tables, in club houses, board rooms, government chambers, locker rooms, classrooms, gymnasiums and church pulpits and pews across America, and until this is faced and fixed, events like those which occurred in Charlottesville will continue to rear their ugly head.

The further truth that was revealed in Charlottesville is that as the so-called alt-right, white supremacy and neo-Nazism are alive and thriving, there will be no progress and overcoming this evil without struggle. Frederick Douglass intimated in the 19th century that there can be no progress without struggle, and that "power concedes nothing without a demand", and Fannie Lou Hamer in the 1950s and 60s similarly asserted that progress comes through perseverance even when we are "sick and tired of being sick and tired."

A place of national lament, reckoning and necessary repentance is found in that it takes tragedies like Charlottesville for people of conscience to begin to raise our collective voices against evil and oppression. The concern is that after the light has fully dimmed on events like Charlottesville, the nation then returns to business, silence and inaction as usual.

As it regards the American Christian churches' complicity with what happened in Charlottesville, and what's likely to happen elsewhere, Jim Wallis in his book *America's Original Sin*, posits that America remains at a point of soul searching and reckoning with its "original sin" - racism. He asserts that "Racism is rooted in sin – or evil, as nonreligious people might prefer – which goes deeper than politics, pointing fingers, partisan maneuvers, blaming and name calling. We can get to a better place only if we go to that morally deeper place.[40] Wallis further asserts, as it regards the Christian church and theology, that "White nationalism is not just racist, it's the anti-Christ."[41]

Michael Eric Dyson posits in his 2017 book, *Tears We Cannot Stop: A Sermon to White America*, that eventually the Christian churches of America (especially white churches) will have to have a Holy conversation about racism in the church and society. The truth of the matter is that a number of the members of the so-called alt-right, KKK, neo-Nazis, 'patriots' and white nationalists who went to Charlottesville in August 2017, raised unholy hell and inflicted unholy violence and death, and many of their sympathizers, worship in "Christian" churches on any given Sunday morning. Over the 244-year history of the nation, while there may have been subtle, episodic hints of such Holy conversation, as it regards race and racism, it

---

[40] Jim Wallis, *America's Original Sin: Racism, White Privilege and the Bridge to a New America* (Grand Rapids, MI: Brazos Press, 2017), 33.
[41] See Jim Wallis, in *Sojourners* (Sojourners, November 27, 2019) and the book *Christ in Crisis: Why We Need to Reclaim Jesus* (New York: HarperCollins, 2019).

has not happened in full measure anywhere, among any Christian denomination or non-denomination. Only when such Holy conversations, and then Holy commitment and engagement, occur in earnest will real racial redemption and reconciliation begin, and only then will Holy transformation occur.

In Montgomery, Alabama, there's a Civil Rights Memorial on the grounds of the Southern Poverty Law Center, designed by Maya Lin, that displays the names of 40 persons of diverse backgrounds, across racial and class lines, who were martyred for the cause of racial and social justice in America. The names on the memorial are representative of thousands of others who have died, and include Emmett Till, Viola Liuzzo, Martin Luther King, Jr., James Reeb, Jimmy Lee Jackson, Addie Mae Collins, Cynthia Wesley, Carole Robertson, Carol Denise McNair, Medgar Evers, Andrew Goodman, James Chaney and Michael Schwerner. It is clear now that the name Heather Heyer, who was killed on that weekend in August 2017 in Charlottesville, became a part of that company of martyred witnesses who died for the cause of freedom and justice for all people.

26 - COLIN KAEPERNICK AND THE PERILOUS POINT OF TAKING A KNEE (An Essay)

Former National Football League player Colin Kaepernick's act of protest in refusing to stand for the playing of the National Anthem, The Star-Spangled Banner, which has traditionally been the practice at the start of NFL games, raises important questions as it pertains to the racial history and current racial climate in America. While they differ in some respects in terms of the contexts in which the two flags were founded and continue to exist, there are interesting parallels that can be drawn between the debates that arose about the Confederate flag in 2016-17, and the Stars and Stripes today - particularly as it pertains to the treatment of Black people in America.

Kaepernick has become the poster example and case in point that to exercise one's First Amendment right to speak and act out on race oppression in America is to risk one's employment. It was clear from the beginning of Kaepernick's taking a knee in 2016 that as right and courageous as he and his cause is, he faced the very real prospect of being blackballed out of the NFL.

This is notwithstanding the fact that he was an NFL starting quarterback through the middle of 2016 before injuries sidelined him, and notwithstanding the fact that less than five years prior to that, he was the starting quarterback and undisputed star on a team that was one play away from winning the Super Bowl. What his being blackballed effectively said is that there were suddenly 64 professional quarterbacks who were better than Kaepernick. It was also interesting to see how his union (the NFL Players Association) did not advocate on his behalf, and only a few of his fellow NFL players acted in solidarity with him.

Concerning flags and their meaning, first, there's the reminder that flags are effectively symbols, and all symbols have meaning. The two flags, the American flag and the Confederate flag, mean different things to different people based on their experience with events and realities that may be attached to them. For many African Americas, the Confederate flag is viewed against the backdrop of the racial history of the nation, and racism that remains a part of the lived experience for many African Americans. As Dr. W.E.B. Dubois intimated in 1903 in *The Souls of Black Folk*, the lived experience of African Americans is one of two-ness - a double consciousness - of being both Black and American. Kaepernick's act of protest reminds us that this two-ness remains as real today as it was over 100 years ago.

The flag debate, and Kaepernick's decision to take a knee is merely an emblem of a deep and very real dis-ease plaguing the nation. It is a dis-ease, which like many others cannot always be seen, but has been extant, malignant and continues to metastasize, often hidden under the surface of the nation. The ongoing killing of black people by police is a manifestation of the racial animus espoused by Donald Trump and his followers.

It is interesting that a U.S. president who avoided military service based on several deferments, and who refused to prove to the people he serves and who pay his salary that he has actually paid taxes over a number of years is the person who most vehemently waved the banner of patriotism and what support of the American flag, and patriotism should look like.

143

Discussion about the disrespect of the American flag by Kaepernick and those who joined him in taking a knee served as distractions from the only stated reason for Kaepernick's decision to take a knee in the first place. He did not take a knee to protest the National Anthem or the American flag, but to protest the fact that scores of Black and Brown people are the victims of police brutality each year, and very few people are being held accountable for such brutality. So, the things that dominated much of the media coverage of Kaepernick centered on labeling athletes who knelt as part of a "black supremacist" movement or as being "un-American".

What is as frightening, disappointing and concerning as the ongoing violence against black bodies by police is the relative silence and inconsistent witness of too many otherwise good people - white, black, brown, red - people who may write and speak loudly at the killing of a black or brown man or woman by police – when it occurs - but who somehow then remain latently silent and inactive until the next killing. The perilous point of Colin Kaepernick's protest, and all that has followed is that what's needed today is a form of consistent, persistent, courageous, audacious, proactive, prophetic moral suasion among people across a wide spectrum of difference, who will have the temerity to speak truth to power and act for the cause of peace with justice in times of relative tranquility just as in times of turmoil, in season and out of season.

27 - *STRENGTH IN A STORM (A Sermon)*

Immediately, Jesus made the disciples get into the boat and go on ahead of him to the other side, while he dismissed the crowd. After he had dismissed them, he went up on a mountainside by himself to pray. Later that night, he was there alone, and the boat was already a considerable distance from land, buffeted by the waves because the wind was against it. Shortly before dawn Jesus went out to them, walking on the lake. When the disciples saw him walking on the lake, they were terrified. "It's a ghost," they said, and cried out in fear. But Jesus immediately said to them: "Take courage! It is I. Don't be afraid." (Matthew 14:22-27)

One of the evidentiary purposes of God in sending God's only begotten Son to earth was to show the world some things. God indeed decided to wrap Godself in human flesh some 2000 years ago, show up as God incarnate, and demonstrate during Jesus's earthly life and ministry that we are never outside the presence of God.

We are never alone. Jesus had another name from his more ancient heritage - *Immanuel* - *God is with us*. This is something that Peter was reminded of one day on a stormy sea. He needed a reminder - a memory lesson - about who Jesus really is. Peter's experience should resonate with some of what we are experiencing *amidst the pandemic storm realities that are ours to live today.*

As it is written in Matthew 14, one night, Peter and the other disciples were sailing across the Sea of Galilee when a strong storm arose. All of a sudden, Jesus showed up walking on water! Naturally, this took the disciples by surprise. *Jesus reassured them: "Take courage! It is I. Don't be afraid"* (Matthew 14:27).

Peter impulsively asked Jesus if he could join Him. He stepped out of the boat and walked toward Jesus. But Peter soon lost focus, became aware of the dangerous and humanly impossible circumstance he was in, and started sinking.

Peter cried out, "Lord, save me!" and *Jesus lovingly reached out his hand, caught Peter, and rescued him* (vv. 30–31).

Many of us might have felt like Peter lately, feeling as though we're sinking amidst the storms we're in, and furthermore feeling as though we're sinking while we try to walk on the turbulent waters of life today.

Indeed, many of us can relate to Peter because we've been on a similar sea lately - crying out to the Lord for help and rescue while we feel like we are sinking - *with the pandemic experiences of isolation and quarantine, concerns for our own health and that of loved ones, worries about financial difficulties, uncertainties about what the future holds.*

The prevailing sentiment of Peter and his fellow disciples was fear. They were frightened... afraid... fearful... scared about what could happen. *And I know that some of us might say that to be afraid is to be unfaithful... that to be afraid is to lack trust in God.*

But I'd like to suggest that to be afraid is to be human. To be afraid is to be true to who we really are in all of our vulnerability and transparency before God. To be afraid is to realize that we are at a point where we can't handle the predicaments before us by ourselves, and we need help.

We will all be afraid from time to time if we are true to ourselves. *And for people who walk by faith and not by sight,* to

146

be afraid is to be at a place where we realize that only with God's help will we get out of the vicissitudinous predicaments we are in. To be afraid and to walk by faith is to walk on the waters of life realizing that Jesus walked on water, and the same Jesus who walked on water 2000 years ago will walk with us today and tomorrow. To be afraid and to walk by faith is to know that Jesus will come to see about us amidst each and every one of the storms that life will bring our way.

What our faith does amidst inevitable fear is it grants us the assurance of a few things –

(1) We are assured that we not alone. Jesus said to Peter and the disciples - *"Take courage! It is I. Don't be afraid".* God's abiding presence gives us the assurance of knowing that we don't journey through the tumultuous seas of life by ourselves. Jesus promised, *"I will never leave you or forsake you. I will be with you always, even to the end of the age"* (Matthew 28:19).

(2) *We are assured that it's all right to ask a God for help.* A faithful act amidst our fears is to ask the Lord for help. Peter cried out as he was sinking on the sea - *"Lord, save me!"* Perhaps, our most faithful act in the pandemic, tsunamic, stormy seasons of our lives is to cry out, pray out to the Lord as Peter did, *"Lord, save us."*

(3) *We are assured that Jesus specializes in saving us.* Jesus reached out his hand, caught Peter, and saved him. Yes indeed, we like Peter can know that Jesus is with us even in the storms of life! Jesus is strength our storms. *He speaks to storms and says "peace", and winds and storms obey him.* He says, *"Let not your hearts be troubled".* Why because he

147

is with us. *Whatever storms come, however long the rain of life might endure, whatever the strength of the winds that come to buffet us, we are never alone.* Jesus is strength in our storms!

> I heard the voice of Jesus saying
> Come into me and rest.
> Lie down thy weary one, lie down
> Thy head upon min breast
> I came to Jesus as I was,
> I was weary, worn and sad.
> And I found in him a resting place,
> And he had made he glad!

SECTION THREE

28– A PRAYER FOR THE STATE OF MARYLAND AND THE MARYLAND STATE SENATE

(This prayer was offered for the Maryland State Senate and State of Maryland, Annapolis, Maryland on Thursday, February 6, 2020.)

O God, you have been our help in ages past, and you are our hope for days to come. We gather today as grateful people, for you have watched over us, and brought us together to do the important work of leading and serving among your people.

Today, we lift up prayers to you for the great state of Maryland, this nation, and the world. We pray for all of those who serve in elected and appointive office on behalf of this state. Bless each of them, O God, with a measure of wisdom, passion, compassion and justice.

O God, we pray today for every city and town represented in these chambers. Bless every school, and every place of work and leisure. Bless your people who are younger and older. And in the ongoing deliberations of this legislative body, let there be careful consideration especially for those in our communities who want for lack of adequate food, shelter, clean water, healthcare and safety.

And in all that you do, O God, in and among us, we will be careful to honor you, and give your name praise. Amen.

29 - JUST MERCY (A Sermon)

With what shall I come before the LORD and bow down before the exalted God? Shall I come before him with burnt offerings, with calves a year old? Will the LORD be pleased with thousands of rams, with ten thousand rivers of oil? Shall I offer my firstborn for my transgression, the fruit of my body for the sin of my soul? He has showed you, O man, what is good. And what does the LORD require of you? To act justly and to love mercy and to walk humbly with your God. (Micah 6:6-8)

As churches gather today, many are like us. We are gathering to worship in Jesus's name. We are gathering to pray and sing, to challenge and encourage one another. We are gathering to hear words of hope and some good news. That's what the church does.

We are doing what we would normally do on a summer Sunday in June (2020). And yet, some things are different. We are gathered not in a physical sanctuary, *but in a cyber sanctuary*. Because of COVID-19, and the need to remain socially distanced, we are virtually connected, but we can't physically touch one another. We are socially and spiritually connected, while we remain physically distant.

Admittedly, preaching and praising through the pandemic is different and difficult. Connecting amidst crisis is challenging. But we take solace in knowing that God meets us in important ways even in storms and tests of our faith and existence.

As we arrive at Micah's prophetic proclamation, we find that Judah was likewise in crisis. Corruption and injustice had permeated their land, and had ravaged the people. As a result of the conditions that they faced, their faith was shaken, and their world was turned upside down and inside out.

We are not the first people to live amidst injustice and unrighteousness, and to have our faith and lives challenged. Judah, too needed a change to come, so that they could re-enter into their next normal, and re-open their lives.

Judah too placed value in the ways and places they had worshipped God. They too found joy and pride in how they had sung songs of Zion, prayed prayers to the Lord their God, and proclaimed God's good news.

In their yearning to meet God in the sanctuary, Micah beckoned them to pause and consider the things that are really important, and what the Lord requires of them.

Micah asked them a question, that contained the answer, *"What does the Lord require of you (people of God), but to do justice, love mercy and walk humbly with God?*

Likewise, what God requires of you and me today is to live lives of humility, and to live in just mercy.

More than ever, I believe that God calls the church to do exactly what Micah told the people of his day that they must do. We are to *do justice, love mercy and walk humbly with God.* More than ever before, God calls us to seek peace and pursue it, seek peace with justice, and love our neighbors as ourselves.

Thirty-one years ago, after graduating from Harvard University, Bryan Stevenson founded the Equal Justice Initiative in Montgomery, Alabama. Since its inception, the Equal Justice Initiative has been about the business of fighting mass incarcerations, and has fought for the exoneration and freedom of over 400 people across America who have been wrongly put on death row. The book and movie, *Just Mercy*, tell the story of Bryan Stevenson and the Equal Justice Initiative in their fight to save hundreds of lives.

In the book, Stevenson writes, "The true measure of our character is how we treat the poor, the disfavored, the accused, the incarcerated and the condemned." He says that there is power in getting proximate with suffering, getting close to suffering as a way to gain deeper understanding and then begin to make change happen.

That is what Jesus did (isn't it?). He was close – proximate - to those who were suffering – the sick, the blind, the dying, the hungry, the imprisoned, the oppressed, the disinherited, and the left out of his day.

Our lives today must be lives that are about the business of seeking *just mercy*. As we move through COVID-19, continue to push for police reform in our communities, advocate for the hurting and hungry, and push for education reform, prison reform and economic justice - God calls us to live lives of *just mercy*.

As we advocate for the well-being of all children, all families, those in all of our communities, Black Lives, and all lives - God calls us to *just mercy*. What does the Lord require of us? *"... to do justice, love mercy, and walk humbly with God."*

O, that we would work so that someday *"justice rolls down as waters, and righteousness as a mighty stream." (Amos 5:24)*

May our prayer be that –
The Lord would lift us up, and let us stand
By faith on Heaven's table (may we) land
(And declare) A higher plane that we have found

We pray that the Lord will plant our feet on Higher Ground.

30 - COVID-19: RACE AND ECONOMICS IN AMERICA

At the emergence of the COVID-19 pandemic in the spring of 2020, I was preparing to teach a graduate-level course on the theology and ethics of Dr. Dietrich Bonhoeffer. I must say that teaching Bonhoeffer has never been a mere academic exercise for me. He was a German Lutheran (Evangelical) pastor-theologian in the 1920s-40s who beckoned his church to confront the evil being inflicted by Adolph Hitler during the Nazi/Aryan/German nationalist regime, which resulted in the deaths of over 10 million Jews, LGBTQI+ persons, Gypsies and other non-Aryans.

As a person of Christian faith - a pastor and theologian - I see parallels with the history of Hitler and Nazi Germany, and what is occurring in America today, especially as it regards the treatment of the poor, working and middle classes, Black and Brown people, and immigrants - with glaring disparities in access to healthcare as has become even more evident during the COVID-19 pandemic, where poor, working and middle class people have lost jobs at unprecedented rates, with the pandemic of ongoing police brutality where Black and Brown people are being killed as though our lives really don't matter much as others, with the precipitous pandemic of white supremacist/nationalist/hate-groups across the nation, and where migrated persons continue to languish and suffer at our borders.

Teaching Bonhoeffer is not a mere academic exercise for me, for as a United Methodist, at our Baptism, we are asked two questions that remain with me in this present moment in the history of God's church and society, *"Do you renounce the spiritual forces of wickedness, and reject the evil powers of this world?", and "Do you accept the freedom and power God gives you to resist evil, injustice, and oppression in whatever forms they present themselves?"*

The 2020 COVID-19 pandemic has shed a bright light on the intersectional crisis of race, economics, and healthcare in America. America has realized yet again what the proverbial saying means that "when America catches a cold, Black and Brown Americans catch pneumonia." African Americans and Hispanics have born a disproportionate brunt of the COVID-19 crisis – disproportionately more jobs lost, less access to adequate healthcare, more death in our families, and more businesses shuttered.

Some persons, including some national leadership, have raised questions as to whether COVID-19 is real, and have claimed that it is a "hoax". In-fact, COVID-19 is a real public health crisis - as scientists, public health experts and healthcare professionals can attest – that is likely to get worse in the coming days, weeks and months. Early and ongoing allegations of a liberal hoax from several right-wing circles, denial of sound/valid medical and scientific evidence, publicity and public relations stunts, political posturing, denial of adequate access to testing, denial of the expansive and actual life-taking and life-threatening effects, and the likely ongoing impact of the virus are the latest evidence of the chaotic, confusing, catastrophic train wreck that we as a nation have fraught upon ourselves.

The reason why Black and Brown Americans know that COVID-19 is real is that in America, the COVID-19 mortality rate is at least 3.6 times higher for Blacks than it is for whites, and the mortality rate is 2.5 times higher for Hispanics than it is for white Americans. Data shows that among seven basic social-political goods - education, employment, healthcare, housing, safety, technology and transportation - there are systemic, persistent, extant racial disparities, inequities and inequalities in these goods' distribution in America. Disparities the distribution and access to these goods intersect, as they all impact each other. The COVID-19 pandemic has shone a glaring light especially on health and healthcare disparities, with exorbitant and disproportionate death rates among Black and Brown people in cities like New York, Chicago, Detroit and New Orleans at 2-3 times the population ratio in those cities and other places.

As of this writing (September 2020) over 200,000 Americans have died from COVID-19, and over 7 million Americans have tested positive for the virus. Indeed, COVID - 19 is so real (and is not a hoax) that it has led to the loss of over one million lives around the world. Part of the tragedy is that this has quickly become another case in point of a failure of national and global leadership, and another clear sign of a willingness to place politics over compassion and concern for the pain and suffering of Americans and others around the world, and to place greed, money and an obsessed concern with America's stock market over planning and preparing for what has become the worst national and global health pandemic of our lifetime.

In light of this, the moral (or amoral) calculus that needs to be taken into consideration in the midst of the debate and push to "re-opening the economy" in the midst of the COVID-19 pandemic is at what and whose cost? Any society that places the value of the stock market over the value of human lives is headed for societal suicide. If the elderly and other at-risk segments of the population are sacrificed at the altar of capitalism today, who is it who will be sacrificed when the next national and global crises occur?

As COVID-19 spread across the nation and globe, there also began to be discussion of the potential need to ration healthcare and equipment like ventilators and other personal protective equipment. A predominant concern for some of us is with how the poor and healthcare insecure/uninsured would be impacted by such rationing if it were to occur. Again, the moral calculus that comes into play is at what and whose cost?

Dr. Martin Luther King intimated something that forever resides with me, and should haunt us all today, and particularly Christians, "There comes a time when silence is betrayal". Similarly, Dr. Bonhoeffer intimated, "Not to speak is to speak, and not to act is to act." And then after lending their voices in renouncing the wickedness and evil of their day, Bonhoeffer and King spoke with their witness in resisting evil, injustice and oppression in the forms that they presented themselves, even unto their early deaths, both at the age of 39. It leaves us to wonder what voice and witness we might be called by God to render today?

31 - WE STAND

(This reflection was given at the Baltimore County Police Reform Rally on July 9, 2020 in Towson, Maryland.)

Today, *we stand* in proxy for those who, because of their deaths, and because they are no longer with us, can no longer stand for themselves.

We stand in proxy for Korryn Gaines, Chris Brown and Freddie Gray. *We stand* in proxy for Ahmaud Arbery, Breonna Taylor, George Floyd and Rayshard Brooks. We stand for Michael Brown, Sandra Bland, Eric Garner and untold others across our region and nation who cannot stand for themselves because they are no longer with us.

We stand in proxy for their loved ones who remain, and must bear the pain and sorrow of no longer seeing or hearing their loved ones. *We stand* in proxy for parents and grandparents who, every day, fear for the safety of their daughters and sons. *We stand* for children who fear for the lives of their parents and grandparents.

We stand because we believe that injustice anywhere is a threat to justice everywhere. *We stand* because we believe that none of us is free unless all of us are free. *We stand* because we believe that violence anywhere is a threat to peace and safety everywhere. *We stand* because we believe that there cannot be true peace without justice.

We stand because we believe that every life is of sacred worth in God's sight. And *we stand as religious communities* because we want to be a part of solutions with our elected and appointed officials, with those persons who police our communities, and with all of those - our businesses, our schools, and our civic organizations that exist in our communities.

We stand because we believe that the great Marylander Frederick Douglass was right when he intimated that there comes a time when all of us must be committed to praying not only with our mouths, but praying with our feet.

We stand because we believe that Black Lives Matter, just as all lives matter. And *we stand* because we believe that we in Baltimore County, and across this region and this great state *can and must do even better.*

We stand because we believe that in order to do better, each of us must commit, with intentionality, temerity and tenacity to doing better. *And we stand* because we believe that if we roll up our sleeves and make change happen - person by person, neighborhood by neighborhood - all of our communities and our people will be better, and all of our communities will be safer.

32 - WE CAN'T BREATHE

This is what the Sovereign Lord says: "Look! I am going to put breath into you and make you live again! (Ezekiel 37:5)

When I played football, there was a phenomenon that would occur only occasionally. But when it occurred, the impact was such that the memory of it would last. Football is a contact sport, and there were a few occasions in my several years of playing where I had the "wind" knocked out of me. For anybody who has ever had the "wind" knocked out of them, they know what it feels like.

When one has the "wind" knocked out of them, the contact is such that they feel for a few moments, like they can't breathe.

The events of these past three months have been like having the "wind" knocked out of us. It has felt as though we as individuals and families, as communities and as a nation and world have had the "wind" knocked out of us. It's felt like we've been punched in our individual and collective gut.

In fact, the last two weeks have felt that we're experiencing a double gut-punch with the lasting and devastating effects of COVID-19, coupled with the brutal death of George Floyd at the knee of a police officer in Minneapolis, Minnesota. Some of Mr. Floyd's last words, as he lay on the ground for 8 minutes, 46 seconds with a knee on his neck, were just three. *"I can't breathe."*

If the truth is told, there are many of us today, as we grieve with the Floyd Family and all those experiencing loss from police violence and other forms of violence, who can relate, *and we feel like we can't breathe.*

In some ways, these three words relate to those we know and those we don't know who have died or have suffered from COVID-19, many on ventilators, unable to breathe. And we are like them in a way, with all that has hit each and every one of us. *We feel like we can't breathe.*

With ongoing economic distress, political unrest and social turmoil, it feels as though we can't breathe. With the uncertainty of our days, it's hard to breathe.

Ezekiel was walking in shoes like yours and mine. He found himself ministering in the midst of proverbial dry bones, with little hope, little possibility, no life. There was little breath in the land. He faced a question as to whether the dry bones of his day could live, whether any breath could come out of the existential death of his day.

And in the midst of breathlessness, God spoke to Ezekiel with a word of promise and possibility for the people of his day. God said, *I am going to put breath back into you and make you live again!*

God said, "You can't breathe right now, but I'm going to put breath in you." God said, "You can't breathe right now, but I am going to make you live again." God said, "You can't breathe right now, but I am a God of new hope, living promise and everlasting possibility."

And God did what God promised to do. God breathed life into the people and their situation 2600 years ago, and the people came alive.

The athlete who gets the "wind" knocked out of them and can't breathe for a moment, eventually gets their "wind" back. *It's called a second "wind".* And when the second "wind" comes, the athlete can play as though they never had the "wind" knocked out of them in the first place.

The same God who breathed life into the people in the days of Ezekiel, can and will give you and me a second wind in the valleys and vicissitudes we now face. The same God who showed up for Ezekiel will breathe on your situation and mine. The same God who breathed when they had no breath, will speak and move again.

The same God who showed up in the people's desperation and desolation in the days of Ezekiel will show up today. The same God who showed up for Israel in their disappointment and despair will show up on in our nation and world today and tomorrow.

Indeed, the God we serve is not dead, and is not done with your life and my life, yet. The same God who kept us yesterday, will keep us today and tomorrow.

Yes, God's breath of everlasting life breathes when we feel that hope is gone.

33 - MINNEAPOLIS: POLICE, PROTEST AND POSSIBILITY

On May 8, 1949, Rev. Dr. Vernon Johns, predecessor to Rev. Dr. Martin Luther King, Jr. at Dexter Avenue Baptist Church, Montgomery, Alabama preached the sermon, "It's Safe to Murder Negroes". I wonder if not the same statement can be made at the sight of the breathtaking death of Mr. George Floyd who died on Monday, May 25, 2020 while in the custody of police officers in Minneapolis, Minnesota, one of whom put a knee on Mr. Floyd's neck for 8 minutes, 46 seconds after he had been detained for attempting to pass a fake $20.00 bill.

While COVID-19 is having devastating effects across the country and world, recent events in Georgia, New York, Louisville, Indianapolis, and Minneapolis are also showing that racialized police brutality, racial profiling and hate-based racial violence are still pervasive across America.

Mr. Floyd's death immediately conjured images of the death of Emmett Till, the fourteen-year-old boy who was lynched in Money, Mississippi on August 28, 1955, as his head was beaten and distorted to an unrecognizable state for the alleged offense of whistling at a white woman. The images of both Mr. Till and Mr. Floyd's deaths are graphic and disturbing.

As Till's death, and disturbing images of his distorted face, raised the ire of much of the nation as it regarded the sin of racism 65 years ago, Floyd's death, and images of a knee on his neck, shed light on the pervasive, pernicious existence of racialized police and pseudo-police violence directed at Black and Brown people in America. Pictures and history tell a tale, from Birmingham, Alabama and the racialized police brutality of Eugene "Bull" Connor and the police of that city in 1963, to Selma, Alabama and the state-sponsored police brutality on the Edmund Pettus Bridge in 1965, to Minneapolis, Minnesota in 2020 - 55 years later.

In the few weeks preceding Floyd's death, Breonna Taylor was ambushed and killed in her home by police in Louisville, Kentucky, Ahmaud Arbery was chased down and shot in the back by racist pseudo-police in Brunswick, Georgia, and a few days after Floyd's death, Rayshard Brooks was shot in the back by police in Atlanta, Georgia.

While the ongoing spate of police-involved killing of black people is a part of a larger narrative of racial animus in America today, and results in ongoing distrust among many Blacks in America of police because of the racial history of state sanctioned violence such as slavery, Jim Crow, lynching, and over-incarceration for relatively minor criminal offenses, a few questions can be raised. First, when is the use of force by police reasonable, and when does it become excessive? How much force is really necessary to subdue and arrest unarmed people? Many of these cases seem to point to the excessive and quick use of lethal force before police try to diffuse and de-escalate tension, and make lawful arrests.

Then, there are concerns with equity. Many people observe an indiscriminate and disproportionate use of lethal force with the arrests of Blacks in contrast to whites. For instance, a white man, Dylan Roof, killed nine people in 2015 at Emmanuel African Methodist Episcopal Church, in Charleston, South Carolina, was arrested relatively peacefully, and was taken to Burger King because he said he was hungry, while unarmed black people are getting beaten and killed by police and pseudo-police for things like selling cigarettes and CDs, carrying Skittles and Arizona Ice Tea, walking and jogging through the wrong neighborhoods, having drugs in their car, or simply running from the police.

In the aftermath of George Floyd's death, and those of Breonna Taylor and Rayshard Brooks there have been protests against police brutality across the nation. The question for some people right now is "Why are they looting?" I experienced it firsthand in DC (1968), Ferguson (2014) and Baltimore (2015), and as a seminary professor, I've worked with dozens of urban ministry students and colleagues in Baltimore doing ethnographic, theo-anthropological and public policy/community engagement work in class and on the ground in the aftermath Baltimore rioting and looting in 2015, trying to arrive at answers to this very question.

Looting is essentially an act rooted in existential and communal anger/rage at persons persistently feeling unheard and forgotten, and in economic deprivation and desperation in being underserved (being poor) by society. Although many of the cases of looting, rioting and protest witnessed in the days following Floyd's death may have support/agitation from outside organized right-wing and left-wing groups, who are complicit and coordinated in tearing up urban space, the looting happened largely in cities where there are large concentrations of Black and Brown, poor and working class people, and not in suburbs and rural areas, where there tend to be smaller concentrations of people of color or persons living in extreme poverty. Thus, there are intersectional race, class and location dimensions to looting. Close attention needs to be paid to the location and kind of – mostly urban, inner city - space that is being destroyed, and who's destroying it, because it will have long-term effects on those who live in and near those urban communities and must stay, while outsiders who are coming in to participate in violent forms of protest and looting have the benefit, privilege and social mobility to leave these cities and return to unaffected suburban, exurban and rural communities after the damage has been done.

This leads to the question of what would be the level of public outcry, disgust, dismay and outrage if 90 percent of the hundreds of persons murdered in cities like Baltimore and Washington, DC over the past 15 years happened to have been young white men and women? Thus, the clarion call of many that "Black Lives Matter, against the backdrop of the people who are talking and acting like black lives are not a part of the 'all'". There continue to be disparate rates of poverty, academic underachievement, under/unemployment, over-incarceration and lack of access to adequate healthcare among Blacks in America. Thus, another question that we must all grapple with is do all of the people who are insisting that 'all lives matter' really mean what they are saying, and do their actions and attitudes match their words? If "all" really does mean "all", and our society reflected it, then and only then would there be no need today for the BLM movement.

An example of what is going on in urban areas across America is what has occurred in Baltimore over the last 15 years. In that city, the murder rate has averaged well over 200 persons per year. The murder rate in DC usually comes in at just over half the number of people killed in Baltimore each year. Over that 15-year period, well over 90 percent of the persons murdered in Baltimore and DC have been African-American males, mostly under age 35. While cases like the deaths of

Freddie Gray, Eric Garner, Sandra Bland and Michael Brown have recently brought to light police brutality against black citizens - the fact of the matter is that the taking of black lives by police and by citizens (including – as is most often the case - the killing of blacks by other blacks) is and has been an ongoing epidemic, especially in major urban centers across America.

Dr. Martin Luther King, Jr. stated that "riots are the language of the unheard", and I'd suggest that riots are also the exercise of power for those who perceive that they are powerless. The more pronounced the perception of powerlessness, the greater the potential for violence. With such perceived and real existential and communal powerlessness, we might continue to see a spate of violent protests similar to what we saw in Los Angeles in 1992, Ferguson in 2014, Baltimore in 2015, and most recently in Minneapolis. Racialized police brutality is a lightening rod, but it's the tip of the iceberg. As Dr. King also intimated, "True peace is not merely the absence of tension, it is the presence of justice."

34 - CONCERNING WHITE FRAGILITY AND CHRISTIAN FAITH

Concerning white fragility and Christian faith, I share with my white sisters and brothers that mature faith means having the conviction and temerity to courageously confront racism for the sin that it is. Anything less than this is fear and complicity. To this day, well-meaning, intelligent, good white people will look at me curiously, and often, I sense, unbelievingly, when I tell them that I pray for my adult son, nephews and all the Black men and boys in my church and community daily, that we will survive when we're stopped by police - anytime, anywhere.

I call my son every week, and I end each call by telling him to please be careful. He knows what that means. It's a brief variation of "the talk" that black parents must have with young black people, as this could be the difference between life and death. As a pastor and professor, I worry about driving home from work at church or school at night, and being stopped (which I have been numerous times over the years), and things not going well, with no cameras turned on, and with no one to witness what could happen.

Why do I pray? Why do I still talk to my adult son? Why do I worry for our lives? It is all because of what happened to George Floyd and others like him who have died while in police custody. It is because the struggle with police brutality targeting Black lives in America is real and pervasive.

One of the reasons we are where we are in America today is because of the minimization by many white people (many of whom, again, I believe to be people of good conscience) of the everyday realities of the problems of race/racism. Such minimization is one of the greatest race traps (and I believe fallacies) that persons fall into, as real issues are seldom addressed, and deep, introspective, hard work is seldom done. As a pastor of mostly black people, I find myself having to provide pastoral care and counseling every day, often several times a day, many times in most weeks, to persons who have had recent experiences with overt and subtle, micro- and macro-aggressive forms of racism and racialized behaviors directed at them, whether at work, in school, while shopping, or at their places of leisure. These are not made up, fantasized stories - but real, painful, extant experiences.

Indeed, African Americans continue to bear the brunt of police brutality, racial profiling and mass incarceration. And these are the ingredients of the recipe for violent protest spreading across the nation in cities, today. The breathtaking, suffocating police-involved killing of George Floyd, and the deaths of many other Black women and men like him at the hands of white police officers and vigilantes also point to a level of moderate, liberal and progressive white guilt, shame and fragility that tends to rise to the surface every time a Floyd or other Black person is killed in such manner. The pattern repeats itself in the aftermath of many of these police-involved killings. There's episodic, apparent white rage among some liberals, progressives and moderates that in short order goes quickly silent and inactive until another George Floyd, Ahmaud Arbery, Breonna Taylor, Trayvon Martin, Sandra Bland, Michael Brown, Philando Castile, Alton Sterling, Korryn Gaines, Eric

Garner, Sean Reed or Freddie Gray dies. What's needed among all persons who seek to be in solidarity with a demand for justice, redress and eradication of the devaluing attacks on Black lives is consistent, persistent, risk-taking, courageous, active voice and presence in this struggle. All else is moral complicity, and such moderation and tolerance are no better than white extremism, nationalism and supremacy.

Martin Luther King, Jr.'s words still ring true, "I have almost reached the regrettable conclusion that the Negro's great stumbling block in his stride toward freedom is not the ku klux klanner, but the white moderate who is more devoted to "order" than to justice." Or as King's friend Abraham Joshua Herschel intimated, "...morally speaking, there is no limit to the concern one must feel for the suffering of human beings, that indifference to evil is worse than evil itself, that in a free society, some are guilty, but all are responsible."

What some of us who are African American beckon our white, and other non-black friends, colleagues, superiors, students, teachers, mentors and mentees to is to do much more in addressing American racism than posting, reposting, liking, tweeting and retweeting famous anti-racism quotes on social media, saying that more needs to be done to overcome racism, going to a cultural competence, diversity or anti-racism workshop, hopping on a webinar to talk about it, reading a book or two on the subject, and seeking consolation and affirmation from their Black friends that they're not racist.

Words mean little if action does not follow. If America's original and most persistent, pernicious sin will ever be fully addressed and eradicated, and if we are to ever move closer to becoming the *Beloved Community,* what's needed is committed, convicted, concerted, consistent, courageous action from a broad spectrum of people. That is what solidarity looks like when it walks and acts in public.

35 - 8 STEPS FOR MOVING FROM PROTEST MOMENT TO SOCIAL ACTION MOVEMENT

(This article was published in Leading Ideas by the Lewis Leadership Center, Wesley Theological Seminary, Washington, DC, July 2020.)

Recent protests in America have heightened awareness regarding several issues affecting persons in our churches and society - from Black Lives Matter and addressing racism and the need for police reform, to the Me Too movement, the Women's March on Washington (2017) and women's rights, to the Never Again movement and demands for comprehensive gun-control in the aftermath of the school shooting at Margery Stoneman Douglas High School in Parkland, Florida in 2018. Questions continue to be raised as to how to bring about substantial, sustainable change in light of public protests around these and other important concerns. In other words, how can protest moments become social action movements?

The story of Nehemiah is a case in point of how social transformation can occur through effective organizing and concerted community action. The first seven chapters of the book of Nehemiah tell the story of the rebuilding of Jerusalem's walls. One notable aspect of the story is that the walls of Jerusalem were rebuilt in 52 days, while the oppression of the people and destruction of Jerusalem had gone on for 141 years. And lessons from the American Civil Rights movement of the 1950s and 60s, the anti-Apartheid and Solidarity and other social reform movements around the world indicate that there are several important principled measures that can be enacted in any community that seeks to bring about sustained, scalable social change as an outcome of public protest.

1. Organize - A key to any movement is organization. Careful early consideration should be given to the people, processes and resources that will be necessary for a movement to address its cause. Every movement is different, but every movement must have organization. One key to organizing is building effective teams, where roles, relationships, responsibilities and expected results are clearly defined. Here, it is important to cast a wide circle of inclusion believing that many persons have experience, gifts and passions that can contribute to a cause. While organizing, it is also important to determine the mission, vision, and purpose (MVP) of the movement. Having a clear MVP serves as a foundation for the seven additional steps.

2. Strategize – Listening to and learning from people with many perspectives is a key to developing a strategy and setting a course for how to go about creating sustained and scalable change. Such listening and learning can often occur with listening sessions and focus groups. Nehemiah recognized the "the trouble we are in" (2:17), and he knew that a movement for change, and the rebuilding of the walls would require proper planning and strategy development. Likewise, during the early days of the Civil Rights movement in Alabama, before and after public protests, strategy sessions would often occur in persons' homes or in churches to determine the best short-term and long-term courses of action.

3. Negotiate – A great deal of change begins and is sustained with wheels that turn behind the scenes. Negotiation should involve all of the stakeholders representing interests that may potentially impact or be impacted by change, and should focus on specific changes that need to occur, and the steps that must be taken. For instance, as an outcome of recent Black Lives Matter protests in Baltimore, a coalition of elected and appointed officials, along with community and religious leaders have met several times, and have been able to negotiate and arrive at proposed police reform legislation for Baltimore County, MD.

4. Mobilize/Implement Change – During the protests for change in Ferguson, Missouri in 2014, after the death of Michael Brown, Leah Gunning Francis in her book *Ferguson and Faith* writes that after protesting and crying out for change to occur, there came a time for persons to "pray with their feet." Mobilizing is the point at which commitment becomes most critical. This is where the people, processes and resources that have been brought together are strategically deployed in the move toward change. Mobilization could involve activities like attending public and private meetings related to a cause, being a part of ongoing negotiating teams, working on communication, public relations and social media, and fundraising.

5. Collaborate – In most social action movements, collaboration is brought about through partnerships among a variety of interests - local elected and appointed government leaders, non-profit, business, community and religious leadership - across ages, genders, races, classes and perspectives. Collaboration typically occurs around common interests among stakeholders to see particular changes occur – whether they be improvements in education, economic development, public safety or other concerns. Collaboration serves as a source of agency, power and synergy in movements as cross-sections of people and resources can often effect greater change together, than can occur if entities operate separately.

6. Evaluate – At various intervals in a movement, it is important to evaluate. Dr. Martin Luther King, Jr. once stated that "change doesn't roll in on the wheels of inevitability." It typically involves hard work, long hours, persistence and sacrifice. The Montgomery Bus boycott, which King helped organize and lead in 1955-56 lasted for 381 days of what was described as days filled with "tired feet and weary souls". Evaluation provides the opportunity for an organization to assess what is working, and what internal changes may need to occur in order to sustain a movement's efforts toward change.

7. Recalibrate - It is easy for groups to lose focus and for people to forget the purpose behind the need for change even in the midst of a movement. As necessary evaluation of successes and challenges occur, there are often points at which recalibration, re-organizing, re-strategizing and redirecting resources (people and finances) become necessary. Such resetting and re-focusing can often help movements sustain and scale, as inevitable external political and social changes may occur that impact the original organization and it plans.

8. Celebrate – In his book, *Crisis in the Village*, Robert M. Franklin writes of the importance of celebrating progress. At points on the journey toward change through social action, it is important to pause and celebrate the change that is occurring. This serves purposes of honoring and encouraging the commitments of those who have been a part of the movement, being building blocks of success and progress upon which to build and take next steps, and being documented historical markers for persons in the future to see what has occurred, and what is possible in the days ahead.

Seasoned leaders know the road to meaningful social change is long and steep. The likelihood of arriving at the desired destination is enhanced when leaders take deliberate steps to transform protest into sustainable social action.

36 - A PRAYER IN A MOMENT OF DIFFICULT DECISION

(Martin Luther King, Jr., offered this prayer at the conclusion of the message "Civilization's Great Need", 1949)

Eternal God out of whose mind
     is the great cosmic universe, we bless thee.
Help us to seek that which is high, noble and Good.
Help us in the moment of difficult decision.
Help us to work with renewed vigor for a warless world,
     a better distribution of wealth,
       and a brotherhood that transcends race or color.

37 - RACE MATTERS (A Sermon)

There is neither Jew nor Gentile, neither slave nor free, nor is there male and female, for you are all one in Christ Jesus. (Galatians 3:28)

To talk about race matters, to be honest and transparent, often feels like being a broken record, standing on the same soap box, and not being able to come down off of it.

But to talk about race matters is to do so because, in America and in the church, race continues to matter. I believe I am at the place where many other persons who provide leadership in various sectors of society are today - whether it be in politics, education, economics, entertainment, sports or religion. We talk about race matters not because we want to, but because we must. We have to talk about it because race still matters.

I told a group of leaders on a webinar a few days ago that all preachers who hope for an inclusive church and society should preach on race matters, because race still matters.

The truth that is ours as a nation is that America was built on the backs, and with the accompanying sweat and brawn, of Black persons who were subjected to the racist institution of American slavery, which lasted for 246 years.

The truth is also that racial politics of redemption and nullification continued to deny rights and opportunities to Black and Brown persons even after slavery had officially ended in 1865.

The truth is also that Dr. Martin Luther King, Jr.'s 57-year-old dream and vision of race and class equality across America, that he shared in his 1963 "I Have a Dream" speech, has gone yet unfulfilled, if his dream has not yet become a nightmare.

The truth is also that the promise of progress that seemed to be on the horizon with President Barack Obama's historic election in November 2007 is an American promise that now seems broken. We must talk about, and reckon with race matters today, because race still matters.

From the ongoing insistence among some persons across America to wave Confederate flags, to resistance of others to removing Confederate monuments of those who perpetuated the evil institution of slavery and promoted secession – it's clear that race still matters.

From maltreatment of immigrants, to ongoing disparities in education, and disparities in accessible, affordable healthcare, employment, income and wealth, race still matters. From disparities in arrests, convictions, sentencing and incarceration of Black abd Brown people in America, race still matters.

So, whatever our lot, if we are faithful and committed to becoming all that God calls us to be, we as the church and society must attend to race matters.

Paul's concerns when addressing the Galatian church and community were concerns that we are well acquainted with today. Paul reminded persons in Galatia that *"There is neither Jew nor Gentile, neither slave nor free, nor is there male and female, for you are all one in Christ Jesus."*

Paul was speaking to very clear distinctions that were being made among God's people based on their social (and by extension, ethnic) identity and caste, based on whether they were Jew or Gentile, slave or free, male or female. That Paul had to speak about oneness and unity is an indication that there was separation and disunity in Galatia.

Paul served notice to religious people in his day, and his message serves notice for us today, that to be in Christ, to be the church, to be the Body of Christ - means we are to have unity - oneness - in Christ.

This is a message that should give us cause to feel challenged and yet to be hopeful. We're challenged today by the fact that even in the church, we're plagued by the reality that Sunday morning remains the most racially segregated hour of the week. We're challenged by the fact that almost all Christians, in almost every church, in almost every neighborhood, in almost every denomination go to church to worship with people who look like them, dress like them, sing like them and pray like them.

Black and Brown Christians are often challenged by the difficulty of trying to live Paul's declaration of oneness in Christ while pushing through the everyday pain of racial aggression and micro-aggressions, and the worry of racial profiling and police brutality where our sons and daughters, grandsons and granddaughters might just be among the next victims.

It is difficult for some of us to see and experience the possibility of the oneness that Paul speaks of amidst the societal and religious separation that continue to plague us. Indeed, race still matters. In her book, *Caste: The Origin of Our Discontent*, Isabel Wilkerson describes America as an "Old house" with a caste system "that is as central to its operation as are the studs and joists that we cannot see in the physical buildings we call home."

And yet hope lies in the promise that God in Christ is well able to bring light out of darkness, love out of hate, joy out of sadness, unity out of separation, and hope out of despair.

Our hope must be rooted in the Lord, who came to break down dividing walls among God's people. Indeed, Christ came to break down dividing walls of racism and classism, dividing walls of hatred and violence.

This is God's plan, God's hope for us. God said through Jeremiah, *"I know plans I have for you, plans for your welfare, and not to harm you, to give you a future with hope"* (Jeremiah 29:11).

God's hope for us is that walls of segregation and separation would be torn down, and bridges of connection -- would be built. God's hope is that walls of division and dissension would fall, and bridges of unity would be built. God's hope is that walls of exclusion would come down, and bridges of inclusion would be built. May it be so.

38 - *LET JUSTICE ROLL (A Sermon)*

But let justice roll down like waters, and righteousness like an ever-flowing stream. (Amos 5:24)

Fifty-seven years ago, next month, on August 28, 1963, Rev. Dr. Martin Luther King, Jr. stood on the steps of the Lincoln Memorial in Washington, DC, one of our national monuments and landmarks, and told America about a dream he had had. King's dream was one where we as a nation would live out the words that are contained in our Declaration of Independence, "We hold these truths to be self-evident that all people are created equal."

On, April 3, 1968, the night before his death in Memphis, Tennessee, King's message to America was framed in a simple request, "All I say to America is, "Be true to what you say on paper."

As we gather to worship here and across the nation on this Independence Day weekend, the evidence indicates that King's dream remains yet unfulfilled, and his request to the nation has gone unattended. In-fact, we are left to wonder today if this Independence Day is an occasion for us to celebrate our nation's freedom, or to lament at the fact that the freedoms of so many Americans are being taken away.

When we sing of this "sweet land of liberty", it has a different tone and texture amidst ongoing police brutality and profiling, and amidst children and families still detained, some separated from each other, on our nation's borders. When we sing of this being "the land of the free and home of the brave", this takes on a different connotation when many cannot clearly see and feel hope in 2020, 244 years after the nation's independence, as many of us can't see an end to racial oppression, economic inequality, social discord, and healthcare disparities, all of which are affecting Brown and Black Americans at exorbitant and disproportionate rates.

When persons pledge our allegiance to the nation, we all declare at the end several telling and aspirational words, "with liberty and justice for all". But what many persons often see and experience is that what this really means is "liberty and justice for some". The real truth lies in the fact that as King intimated, *"injustice anywhere is a threat to justice everywhere."* The real truth lies in the fact that *none of us are free unless all of us are free.*

The prophet Amos preached to similar concerns about the injustice that the people of his day experienced. Amos implored the people of his day to *"let justice roll down as waters, and righteousness as a mighty stream".*

To get the gist of the "what" and the "why" of the prophet's words about justice rolling, we can look at two concerns that Amos had for the people of his day. The first concern was that there were a lot of religious people in Israel, but there weren't enough who were righteousness.

If Amos were with us today, he would observe that the "lack" of religion is not our problem. We can find religion on every corner. We can find churches in almost every neighborhood in America. We can find all the religion we want on the internet or on television. There's no scarcity of religion, but if Amos were with us today, he would observe, like some of us observe that *in light of all of our religion, we need more righteousness.* That's why Amos implored the people to whom he was preaching to let *"righteousness flow as a mighty, everlasting stream."*

We need more people, who, in light of our religion, walk in God's righteousness. We need more people today, *who, in light of our religious rituals, have a right relationship with God,* and by virtue of that, know how treat our neighbors right.

And this gets to Amos's second, and corollary concern, and what justice and righteousness look like when they speak out loud, and walk in public. Amos's primary concern with the injustice and unrighteousness of his day was with how society was treating the poor, oppressed and marginalized people of that day. In chapter 2, Amos said that *"they sell the righteous poor for silver and the needy for a pair of shoes."* In other words, they were selling people into debt slavery for owing as little as the price of shoes.

God was concerned then, and God is concerned today, with how each of those who have the least among us is treated. Amos's prophetic warning to the people of his day was that if the people could not and would not attain to justice and righteousness, as expressed in their concern for the poor and oppressed (all of God's people), they would be wiped out.

Two of my favorite places in the world to go are Niagara Falls in upstate New York and Canada, and Victoria Falls in Zimbabwe in southern Africa. Both sets of falls are natural wonders, and reminders of the splendor of God, God's majestic power. Mighty water falls in both places, and the water falls as it has for thousands of years. Mighty water falls as only God can make it fall.

So, the encouragement for you and me, the encouragement for the church and the world today is to let justice and righteousness roll as mighty waters in our lives.

Let justice roll in every community.

Let justice roll in every city and state.

Let it roll for every woman and man, girl and boy.

Let it roll for black, brown and white persons.

Let it roll for richer and poorer.

Let justice roll for immigrants.

Let justice roll until racism and classism are annihilated.

Let justice roll until we see as Jesus hoped and preached
that those who are blind will see,

those who are bound and oppressed are liberated,

and those who are poor experience all of the goodness of
the Lord.

Let Justice roll!

39– A PROPOSITION OF PANDEMIC POSSIBILITY

"When you pass through the waters, I will be with you; and when you pass through the rivers, they will not sweep over you. When you walk through the fire, you will not be burned; the flames will not set you ablaze." (Isaiah 43:2)

(This sermon was preached at Oxnam Chapel, Wesley Theological Seminary, Washington, DC on October 6, 2020)

Facing the devastating effects of danger and distress, the Israelites were in need of a word from the Lord. They were living through some kind of existential hell, drowning in a sea of despair. We don't know exactly what their troubles were, but we know is that they were in trouble.

How do we know this? We know because there would have been no other reason for Isaiah to offer such words of comfort and encouragement.

Let's hear Isaiah talk to his people with these words from the Lord: *"When you pass through the waters, I will be with you; and when you pass through the rivers, they will not sweep over you. When you walk through the fire, you will not be burned; the flames will not set you ablaze."*

Isaiah could have just as easily given them the remixed, Baltimore, 2020 version of God's promise - and told them that "come hell or high water, God has made a promise that God will be with you."

I know this sounds rather crass and raw, and maybe not that religious and holy, but this is a word for those of us who awakened today wondering how we're going to deal with the hell and high waters of our lives.

So, it might serve us well to take heed of Isaiah's use of the metaphors of going through high waters and blazing fires to consider the trials that we are facing or will face, and the difficulties that we are going through and will go through.

One important thing to notice about Isaiah's words to the people of his day is that he used the words *"when you go through..."* Isaiah didn't use words of conjecture, possibility or probability - he didn't say to them *"if you go through"* or *"in the event you go through"* or *"in case you go through"*. Isaiah used words of certainty and inevitability - *"when you go through"*.

This is a word for *when we go through* high waters and *when we face* fires in our lives... when death knocks on our door... when sickness comes... when brokenness in relationships occurs... when broken minds, broken spirits and broken hearts are ours. Isaiah is speaking of times *when we go through.*

What people of faith need in this present age are real promises of how God is going to help us wade through the inevitable high waters, and deal with the real pain many of us are experiencing. We need a word from the Lord that speaks to how we are going to wade through the high waters and come out of COVID-19, and how some of us, or some of those we know, are going to wade through the high waters of wondering what we will eat and where we will live.

As Isaiah offered a proposition of pandemic possibility to the people of his day, we need a similar word from the Lord that speaks promise, possibility and hope of how we are going to wade through the high waters of concern for over 40 million people in America who have lost their livelihoods, and tens of thousands more who have lost their lives due to COVID-19. We need assurance from God amidst the high waters of race animus in our midst, where we still have to wonder whether Black lives really do matter. We need a word from the Lord amidst the high waters of the real concerns that we have for our children and grandchildren's future.

Isaiah wrote this song of hope and promise to his people about 2700 years ago as they were facing similar high waters of uncertainty - wondering about their future, and wondering if and when God was going to show up for them.

Indeed, we are not the first people to face the predicament of hell and high waters. We're not the first generation to be steeped in apparently overwhelming and insurmountable odds. We're not the first people to encounter mountains of despair and valleys of vicissitudinous disappointment.

Isaiah wanted the people to know that *the same God* who delivered their parents from the high waters of the Red Sea 1000 years before, would bring them through the high waters they were facing. *The same God* who met their ancestors at the banks of the chilly Jordan river would come to see about them.

The same God who would deliver Meshach, Shadrach and Abednego from a fiery furnace would bring them out of the fires they were facing.

And we can rest assured today that *the same God* who brought generations before ours through difficult days, will bring us through today and tomorrow.

- The same God who the Israelites called *Jehovah Niche* is the same God who protects us today.
- The same God who they called *Jehovah Jireh* will provide for us.

- The same God who they called *Jehovah Raphe* heals today.
- The same God who they called *Jehovah Shalom* brings peace today.
- The same God who was an on-time God 2700 years ago, in Isaiah's day, is an on-time, every time, all-the-time God today.

"When you pass through the waters, I will be with you; and when you pass through the rivers, they will not sweep over you. When you walk through the fire, you will not be burned; the flames will not set you ablaze."

Indeed, Isaiah offered the people to whom he was preaching a proposition of pandemic possibility to remind them that God is a very present help in times of trouble. He wanted them to know that the God they served, and the Christ we know will never leave us or forsake us.

We can rest assured that whatever the storms of life that rage, Jesus will stand by us.

When the world is tossing you and me like a ship upon the sea, God who rules winds and waters will stand by us. (Rev. Charles Albert Tindley)

40 - THE POWER OF PENTECOST (A Sermon)

"But you will receive power when the Holy Spirit comes on you; and you will be my witnesses in Jerusalem, and in all Judea and Samaria, and to the ends of the earth." (Acts 1:8)

By all measures, these are unprecedented times in our lives. With the reality of a global health pandemic, necessary quarantine and isolation, economic stress and distress, political corruption and disruption, social unrest and dis-ease, police brutality, and the persistent, pernicious, horrific, heinous attacks on Black lives, many of us are left to feel powerless today.

Indeed, images of a police knee on the neck of a Black man, George Floyd in Minneapolis, images of Ahmaud Arbery, a Black man shot in his back while jogging in Georgia, images of thousands of people who struggle to breathe on their backs, on ventilators, because of a virus that seems more powerful than any of us, we are left to wonder what power there is to make things better.

If Pentecost is about anything, it is about the power of God. Indeed, God is yet true to God's promises. We find in Acts 1:8, that Jesus said *"But you will receive power when the Holy Spirit comes on you; and you will be my witnesses in Jerusalem, and in all Judea and Samaria, and to the ends of the earth."*

This power of God, the Holy Ghost, the spirit of God beckons us to see and believe - as difficult as things are - whatever we're going through, that God has power to bring us through, and that God will somehow, someway, someday get us through.

The Pentecostal power of God is what our faith and hope must rest on in these trying times. The Pentecostal power of God means, for those of us who walk by faith and not by sight, that we know of and must rely on a higher power than ourselves, our governments, and even our church institutions.

Pentecostal power is that which John talked about when he told the church in Jerusalem that *"Greater is God who is in us, than he that is in the world."* Indeed, these days beckon us to call on Pentecostal power.

It is the power that Paul talked about to those in Ephesus when he said *"Now unto God who is able to do exceedingly and abundantly above all that we could ask or think according to the power that is in us."* (Ephesians 20-21)

It is the same power that Paul talked about again when he told his protégé Timothy that *"God has not given us the spirit of fear, but of power, love, sound mind."* (2 Timothy 1:7)

The Holy Spirit, the Spirit of the living God, is that which must empower the church and world today. It is that which helps us to love our neighbors and our enemies. It is that which helps us pray for one another. It is that which helps us treat each other right. It's that which helps us to serve the common good.

It is that which makes us work for peace with justice. It is that which makes us fight for right *until justice rolls down as waters, and righteousness as a mighty stream.* It is that which makes us *love mercy, do justice and walk humbly with God.* It is that which gives us strength to struggle until racism is eradicated and sexism are expunged, until classism, xenophobia and homophobia are eliminated, until hate and malice are no more.

It is urgent that we as people of faith in the all-mighty God - the Church, the family of God - see that it is the power of God – Pentecostal power - that can and must make America and its Christian Church overcome its most daunting and dreadful sin, the sin of racism.

If we are in Christ, we will commit ourselves to working to overcome racism that results in racial violence by police and white vigilantes, racism that results in separation of families at our borders, racism that leads to racial profiling, and racism that results in disparities in healthcare, housing, employment and incarceration for Black and Brown people in America.

It is urgent that we see that Jesus's primary intent was to preach good news the poor, and set at liberty those shackled by oppression in his day. And if we are to be followers of Jesus - followers of the way, our concern must likewise be for the oppressed and disinherited among us.

May it be that the Power of Pentecost – Pentecostal Power – will be in each and every one of us - Black and White, poor and rich, female and male. May the ushering in of such power be our prayer today and until kin-dom comes.

41 - *THE BENEDICTION - I NEED YOU*
(By Howard Thurman)

I need Your sense of time. Always I have an underlying anxiety about things. Sometimes I am in a hurry to achieve my ends and am completely without patience. It is hard for me to realize that some growth is slow, that not all processes are swift. I cannot discriminate between what takes time to develop and what can be rushed because my sense of time is dulled. O to understand the meaning of perspective that I may do all things with a profound sense of leisure of time.

I need Your sense of order. The confusion of the details of living is sometimes overwhelming. The little things keep getting in my way, providing ready-made excuses for failure to do and be what I know I ought to do and be. Much time is spent on things that are not very important while significant things are put in an insignificant place in my scheme of order. I must unscramble my affairs so that my life will become order. O God, I need Your sense of order.

I need Your sense of the future. Teach me to know that life is ever on the side of the future. Keep alive in me the future look, the high hope. Let me not be frozen either by the past or the present. Grant me, O Patient One, Your sense of the future without which all life would sicken and die.

ABOUT THE AUTHOR

A native of Washington D.C., Rev. Dr. C. Anthony Hunt is the Senior Pastor of Epworth Chapel United Methodist Church in Baltimore, MD, and is Professor of Systematic, Moral and Practical Theology and Permanent Dunning Distinguished Lecturer at the Ecumenical Institute of Theology, St. Mary's Seminary and University in Baltimore. He also teaches at Wesley Theological Seminary in Washington, DC, United Theological Seminary in Dayton, OH, and the Graduate Theological Foundation in Oklahoma City, OK, where he is a Faculty Fellow and E. Franklin Frazier Professor of African-American Studies.

A graduate of the University of Maryland, he holds advanced degrees from Troy State University, Wesley Theological Seminary and the Graduate Theological Foundation. Additionally, he has completed post-graduate studies at the Center of Theological Inquiry, Princeton, NJ; the University of Oxford, UK; St. Mary's Seminary and University, Baltimore, MD; Bethel University, St. Paul, MN; and the Institute of Certified Professional Managers, James Madison University, Harrisonburg, Va. He is an inductee in the Rev. Dr. Martin Luther King, Jr. International Board of Preachers at Morehouse College, Atlanta, GA.

He is the author of eleven other books including, *Songs for the Seasons: Sermons on the Psalms, vol. 2* (2020); *I've Seen the Promised Land: Martin Luther King, Jr. and the 21st Century Quest for the Beloved Community* (2020); *Come Go with Me: Howard Thurman and a Gospel of Radical Inclusivity*

(2019); and *Stones of Hope: Essays, Sermons and Prayers on Religion and Race, vol. 3* (2017); and over 175 articles, chapters and academic papers on matters pertaining to religion and society.